MINKAL VAISHNAV

Past Life DOWSING

TRANSFORM YOUR PAST, ELEVATE YOUR LIFE
WITH 41 PENDULUM HEALING SESSIONS

DISCLAIMER

This publication is designed to provide metaphysical information regarding the spiritual matter. It is offered with the understanding that the author and publisher are not engaged in rendering medical or psychological service. The information in this book is for educational purposes only. This book is not intended to be a substitute for professional, medical advice or therapy.

"As we heal the echoes of our past lives, we dissolve the chains that bind us to old cycles. In this liberation, we awaken to the true essence of our being, free to create a life filled with love, growth, and infinite possibilities."

CONTENT

ABOUT THE BOOK

Past life healing is a process that involves exploring and addressing unresolved issues, traumas, or patterns from previous lifetimes that continue to influence your current life. The concept is based on the belief that our souls carry memories, emotions, and energies from past incarnations, which can manifest as recurring challenges, fears, or limiting beliefs in our present existence.

The correlation between healing the past and its impact on the present and future is deeply intertwined, as all aspects of time are connected in the continuum of our soul's journey. When we heal past wounds, traumas, or unresolved issues, we do more than just address the remnants of old experiences - we create ripples that affect both our present and future.

HEALING THE PAST:

Our past, whether in this lifetime or previous ones, shapes who we are today. Unresolved emotions, fears, and patterns from the past can manifest in our current life as recurring challenges, limiting beliefs, or emotional blocks. By consciously healing these aspects of the past, we release the energetic imprints that have carried over into the present. This healing allows us to free ourselves from repeating cycles and to experience life with greater clarity, peace, and alignment with our true essence.

IMPACT ON THE PRESENT:

When we heal the past, we transform the lens through which we view and interact with the world. The emotional and energetic weight that once held us back is lifted, allowing us to make decisions and take actions from a place of empowerment rather than fear or limitation. The present moment becomes more vibrant and full of potential as we are no longer bound by the shadows of the past. We can fully engage with life, embrace opportunities, and cultivate deeper relationships with ourselves and others.

SHAPING THE FUTURE:

The future is not a fixed destination but a field of possibilities influenced by our current state of being. By healing the past, we shift our energy and consciousness in the present, which in turn shapes the trajectory of our future. A healed past allows us to project a future that is unencumbered by old patterns and filled with new possibilities. The future we create becomes a reflection of our healed and empowered self, where we can manifest our highest potential and live a life aligned with our true purpose.

In essence, healing the past is an act of self-liberation that reverberates through time. It brings harmony to our entire being, creating a balanced and empowered present while paving the way for a future that is bright, expansive, and filled with limitless possibilities. By addressing the past, we not only heal our present but also consciously craft a future that is aligned with our highest good and the fulfillment of our soul's journey.

This book offers 41 specialized dowsing sessions centered on past life healing, each tailored to support your journey of healing and transformation.

This book will help you embark on a profound journey into past life healing, guiding you to delve into the depths of your soul and unravel the threads that bind you to patterns and experiences from long ago. Each session in this book is designed to help you uncover and address the memories, emotions, and energies from past lives that subtly influence your present existence. By consciously working through these echoes of the past, this book unlocks the potential for you to release burdens that no longer serve you, creating space for growth, joy, and fulfillment in your current life.

As you engage with the healing sessions in this book, you won't just be addressing old wounds - you'll be reclaiming lost fragments of your soul. These fragments, scattered across time and space, hold the essence of who you are at your core. By reintegrating them, you'll become more whole, more aligned with your true purpose, and more capable of manifesting your highest potential. The healing process outlined in this book transcends time, bringing harmony to your past, present, and future, and allowing you to live more fully in the now.

The beauty of working with this book lies in its ability to help you transform darkness into light. Every scar from a past life is a symbol of a lesson learned, an experience endured, and wisdom gained. Through the healing sessions, you will turn these scars into guiding lights that illuminate your path forward. This transformative process not only heals you but also contributes to the healing of the collective consciousness, raising the vibration of all beings connected to you across time.

By embracing the healing techniques in this book, you'll acknowledge that your journey is one of eternal growth, where every experience, no matter how challenging, serves a purpose in the grand tapestry of your soul's evolution. By healing your past, you empower yourself to create a future unburdened by old patterns, free to express your truest, most radiant self. This journey is about reclaiming your power and transforming old wounds into the foundation upon which you can build a life of love, light, and limitless potential.

HOW TO USE THIS BOOK!

This book is designed to help you explore past life wounds and bring healing to the present and future through 41 dowsing worksheets, each focused on a unique past life healing concept. By working with these worksheets, you can identify and clear energetic patterns, unresolved traumas, or karmic influences that may be affecting your current life.

- Go through all the dowsing sessions to familiarize with various past life healing concepts and strategies for inner work and exploration.

- For an intuitive personalized approach you can start with the four charts and pick the right sessions to begin your past life journey.

Everything you need is already within you. The answers you are searching for, the guidance you seek, and the clarity you desire are all waiting for you to recognize and embrace them. This book, with its dowsing charts and worksheets, is a tool to help you uncover those inner truths.

USING THE CHARTS TO REVEAL YOUR PATH

Through these charts, you can tap into your inner wisdom and receive the messages you need to work on your life. Each chart and dowsing session serves as a mirror, reflecting the insights and answers that are already present within you, waiting to be acknowledged.

Trust the movement of the pendulum to guide you to the right session or concept. Trust your intuition and the guidance you receive through the pendulum.

Be open to the messages you receive, even if they are unexpected or seem unrelated at first glance. Often, the insights we need come in surprising ways.

By using these charts, you're not just looking for answers outside of yourself - you're allowing the tools in this book to help you access the deep wisdom, knowledge, and healing power that already resides within you. Trust that the answers you need are already there, waiting for you to discover them.

Remember that healing can take time and may require multiple sessions. Be patient and gentle with yourself as you progress through your healing journey.

Here are the steps for working with a chart.

IDENTIFY THE ISSUE:

- Reflect on the specific issue or situation you want to address. This could be anything from a relationship challenge, a health concern, an emotional blockage, or a spiritual question.

- Write down the issue or situation in your journal. Be as specific as possible to help you focus during the dowsing process.

REVIEW THE FOUR CHARTS:

The book includes four charts, each corresponding to a different aspect of healing.

1. Life Healing
2. Relationships and Wealth Healing,
3. Mind-Body-Emotions Healing,
4. Spiritual Healing.

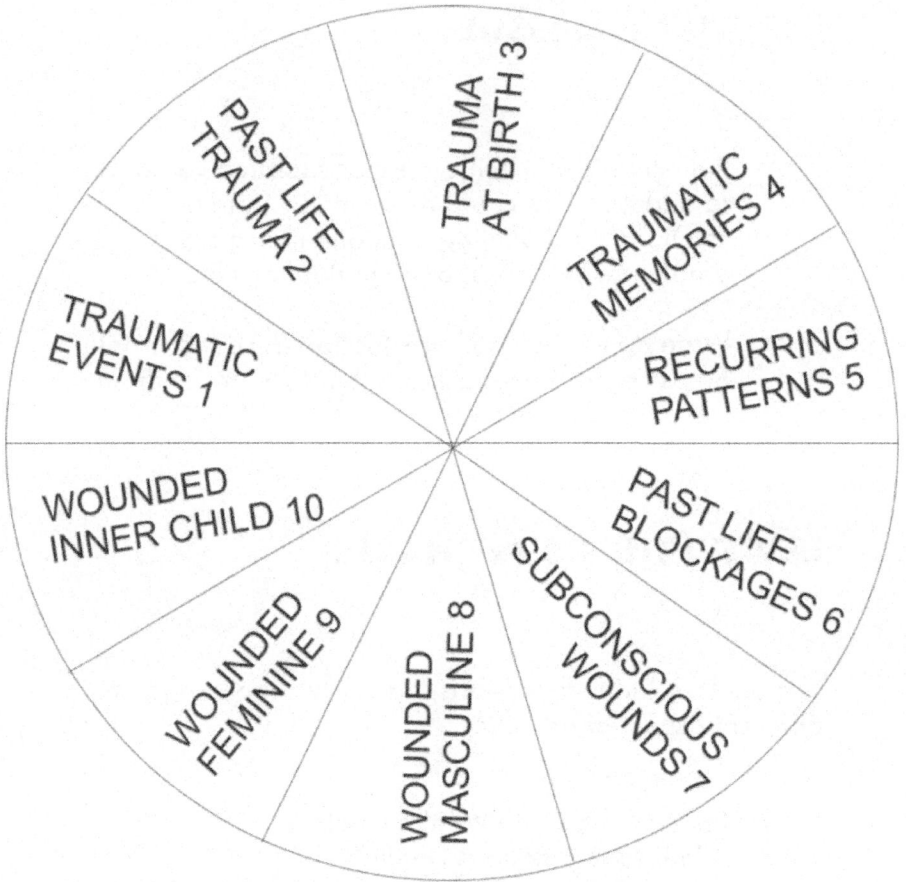

CHART 1: LIFE HEALING

ASK KEY QUESTIONS:

Hold your pendulum over the chart, and ask,

- "Which past life session will most benefit me?"
- "Which issue do I need to work upon?"
- "What is good for me to do?"
- "Which past life session do I need to take?"
- "Which past life session is best for me?"
- "Which past life session is suitable for me?"
- "What do I need to do about this situation?"

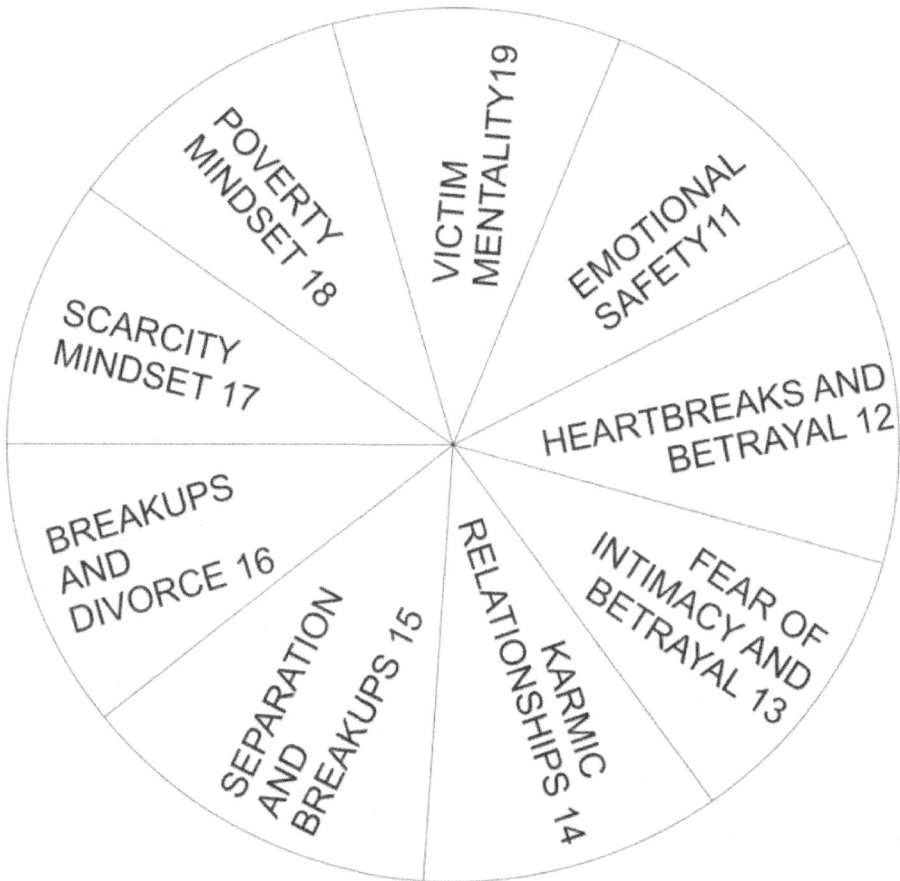

CHART 2: RELATIONSHIPS AND WEALTH

ASK KEY QUESTIONS:

Hold your pendulum over the chart, and ask,

- "Which past life session will most benefit me?"
- "Which issue do I need to work upon?"
- "What is good for me to do?"
- "Which past life session do I need to take?"
- "Which past life session is best for me?"
- "Which past life session is suitable for me?"
- "What do I need to do about this situation?"

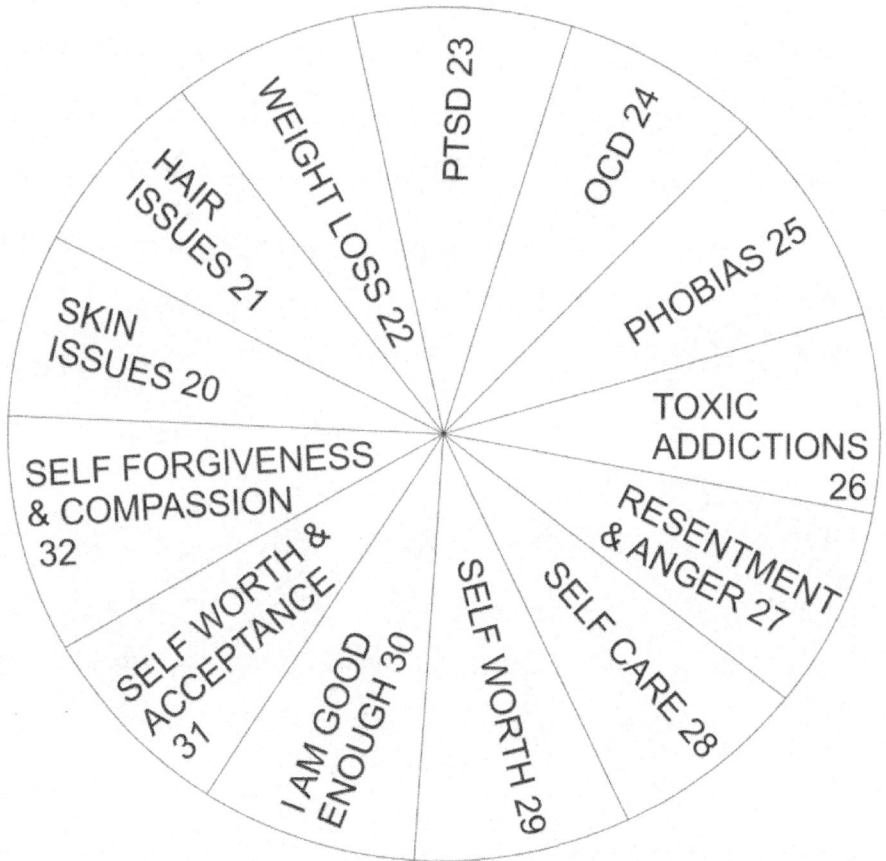

CHART 3: MIND, BODY EMOTIONS

ASK KEY QUESTIONS:

Hold your pendulum over the chart, and ask,

- "Which past life session will most benefit me?"
- "Which issue do I need to work upon?"
- "What is good for me to do?"
- "Which past life session do I need to take?"
- "Which past life session is best for me?"
- "Which past life session is suitable for me?"
- "What do I need to do about this situation?"

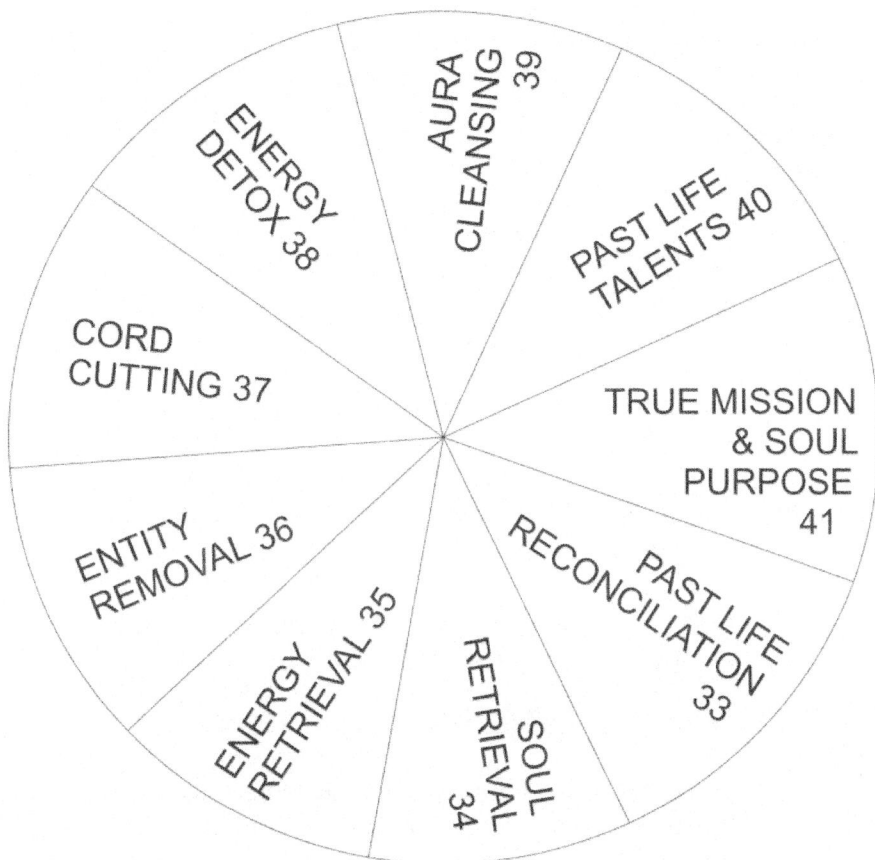

CHART 4: SPIRITUAL HEALING

ASK KEY QUESTIONS:

Hold your pendulum over the chart, and ask,

- "Which past life session will most benefit me?"
- "Which issue do I need to work upon?"
- "What is good for me to do?"
- "Which past life session do I need to take?"
- "Which past life session is best for me?"
- "Which past life session is suitable for me?"
- "What do I need to do about this situation?"

ARRANGE THEM IN ORDER:

Make a list of the sessions you need to work to heal a particular issue and organize them in rank based on top priority.

- Is there a specific order in which I should complete the sessions?

- Which session should I do first? Which next?

- "What step should I take next for my highest good?"

- How many sessions do I need to work on to fully resolve this issue?

- Is there any specific time or day that would be most beneficial for these healing sessions?

SELECT YOUR DOWSING SESSION:

- Once you have your sessions identified, turn to the corresponding section in the book. Go through the session step-by-step, following the dowsing commands and engaging fully with the process. Visualize the energy shifts, clearings, and healings as you proceed.

- Depending on the issue, you may need to revisit the session multiple times. Regular practice can lead to deeper and more lasting healing.

- As you continue your healing journey, periodically return to the charts to ask if there are new issues to address or if further work is needed on the same issue.

REFLECT AND INTEGRATE:

After completing the sessions, check in with yourself to assess if the issue has been resolved or if further healing is necessary.

1. "Is the issue resolved now?"

2. Do I need to repeat any of the sessions for deeper healing? If so, which ones?

Reflect on how the session relates to your current issue. Sometimes the connection might be straightforward; other times, it might require deeper contemplation to understand how it applies.

After completing the dowsing session, take a few moments to reflect on your experience. What insights or shifts did you notice?

Write down any thoughts, feelings, or realizations that arose during the session. This can help you track your progress and identify patterns over time.

FOLLOW UP:

Healing is often a layered process, so revisit the charts and sessions regularly to check your progress or address new issues as they arise.

Keep asking the key questions:

- "Which session will most benefit me now?"

- "What is good for me to do next?"

INTERPRET THE SESSIONS WITH FLEXIBILITY

- While working with the charts, you may receive a session that is directly applicable to your issue, or one that doesn't seem immediately relevant. In cases where the session doesn't directly apply, look deeper into the technique or strategy provided. Sometimes, a specific affirmation, command, or concept from that session is exactly what you need to stabilize or complete your healing.

- Remember, the healing process is not always linear. Be open to the possibility that even an unexpected session may hold the key to resolving your current challenges. Trust in the guidance you receive, and allow yourself to go with the flow.

INTEGRATE THE HEALING INTUITIVELY

- Use your intuition to fully integrate the healing. You might feel drawn to combine elements from different sessions, use specific commands or affirmations repeatedly, or explore a particular concept more deeply. Pay attention to your inner guidance and allow it to shape your healing journey. Each step you take is an important part of aligning your past, present, and future for your highest good.

- By embracing this flexible, intuitive approach, you can make the most of the book and its resources, ensuring that your past life healing journey is deeply personalized and effective.

CELEBRATE YOUR PROGRESS:

Acknowledge and celebrate the shifts and changes you experience, no matter how small they may seem. Recognizing progress builds confidence and reinforces positive changes.

By engaging fully with each chart, you create a personalized healing journey that aligns with your unique needs and circumstances, allowing you to transform and elevate your life experience.

ALL ABOUT PENDULUM DOWSING

WHAT MAKES PENDULUM DOWSING SPECIAL?

Pendulum dowsing is a unique and versatile practice that combines intuition, energy work, and spiritual guidance. Here are some key aspects that make pendulum dowsing special:

DIRECT CONNECTION TO INTUITION

- **ENHANCES INNER GUIDANCE:**

  Pendulum dowsing allows you to tap directly into your intuition and subconscious mind. It serves as a bridge between your conscious awareness and your inner wisdom, helping you access answers and insights that may not be immediately obvious.

- **EMPOWERS SELF-DISCOVERY:**

  By working with a pendulum, you can explore your thoughts, feelings, and beliefs in a deeper, more reflective way. This practice helps you cultivate a stronger sense of self-awareness and trust in your inner voice.

ACCESSIBLE AND EASY TO LEARN

▪ SIMPLE TO USE:

Pendulum dowsing requires minimal tools - a pendulum and a calm, focused mind. It doesn't require any specialized training, and with practice, anyone can learn to use a pendulum effectively.

▪ PORTABLE AND CONVENIENT:

A pendulum is small and portable, making it easy to carry and use anywhere. Whether at home, outdoors, or traveling, you can access its guidance whenever you need it.

VERSATILITY IN APPLICATIONS

▪ WIDE RANGE OF USES:

Pendulum dowsing can be used for various purposes, including decision-making, energy healing, manifesting, clearing blockages, finding lost objects, and exploring spiritual questions. Its versatility makes it a valuable tool in many aspects of life.

▪ CUSTOMIZABLE TO YOUR NEEDS:

You can adapt pendulum dowsing to suit your specific goals, whether for personal growth, emotional healing, relationship guidance, or enhancing your spiritual practice.

ENHANCES SPIRITUAL AND ENERGY WORK

- ## SUPPORTS ENERGY HEALING:

  Pendulum dowsing can be used to detect and balance energy fields, clear chakras, and release emotional blockages. It's a valuable tool for energy healers, Reiki practitioners, and anyone interested in promoting holistic well-being.

- ## DEEPENS SPIRITUAL CONNECTION:

  By using a pendulum, you can connect with your higher self, spiritual guides, angels, or other benevolent entities. This practice can enhance your spiritual growth and foster a deeper sense of connection to the universe.

PROMOTES MINDFULNESS AND FOCUS

- ## CULTIVATES PRESENCE:

  Dowsing requires you to be present and focused in the moment, which can help develop mindfulness. By concentrating on the pendulum's movements and your inner questions, you naturally enter a meditative state that calms the mind and reduces stress.

- ## ENCOURAGES REFLECTION:

  The practice of formulating clear, specific questions for the pendulum encourages thoughtful reflection on your situation, helping you gain clarity and perspective.

NON-INVASIVE AND SAFE

▪ GENTLE AND NON-INVASIVE:

Unlike some other forms of divination or spiritual practice, pendulum dowsing is gentle and non-invasive. It does not require altering your state of consciousness significantly or involving any external substances or tools that might carry risks.

▪ ACCESSIBLE TO EVERYONE:

People of all ages and backgrounds can use pendulum dowsing, making it an inclusive practice that can be tailored to fit individual beliefs, needs, and comfort levels.

ENCOURAGES PERSONAL EMPOWERMENT

▪ FOSTERS INDEPENDENCE:

Pendulum dowsing empowers you to seek answers and solutions within yourself rather than relying solely on external sources. It encourages self-trust and independence, helping you to take ownership of your decisions and path.

▪ FACILITATES PERSONAL HEALING:

Dowsing can be a powerful tool for self-healing. By identifying and addressing negative beliefs, emotional blockages, or past traumas, you can initiate your own healing processes and move toward greater well-being.

RESONATES WITH NATURAL ENERGIES

▪ ALIGNS WITH EARTH ENERGIES:

Pendulum dowsing has roots in ancient practices that recognize the subtle energies present in the earth and the human body. It resonates with the natural rhythms and vibrations of the environment, making it a holistic and grounded practice.

▪ BALANCES PERSONAL ENERGIES:

Working with a pendulum can help you balance your energy fields (like the aura and chakras) by identifying and clearing energy imbalances or blockages. This balancing can enhance physical, emotional, and spiritual well-being.

PROVIDES IMMEDIATE FEEDBACK

▪ INSTANT RESPONSES:

Unlike some other divination tools that require interpretation or a waiting period, a pendulum provides immediate feedback. Its movements - whether circular, linear, or still - give direct answers to your questions, making it a quick way to gain insights.

▪ CONTINUOUS COMMUNICATION:

You can ask multiple questions in one session and get continuous feedback. This makes it ideal for situations where you need quick guidance or have several related inquiries.

ACTS AS A SPIRITUAL COMPANION

▪ PERSONALIZED TOOL:

Your pendulum becomes a personalized tool that reflects your unique energy signature. The more you use it, the more it aligns with your frequency, making it a trusted companion for spiritual exploration and daily decision-making.

▪ STRENGTHENS SPIRITUAL DISCIPLINE:

Regular pendulum practice can help establish a routine for spiritual discipline, encouraging you to connect with your inner self and higher consciousness consistently.

FACILITATES PAST LIFE EXPLORATION AND HEALING

▪ EXPLORES DEEP-SEATED ISSUES:

Pendulum dowsing can be used to explore past life experiences, revealing karmic patterns, unresolved traumas, or past-life influences that affect your current life.

▪ SUPPORTS TRANSFORMATIONAL HEALING:

By identifying past life issues, pendulum dowsing provides an opportunity for deep, transformational healing that aligns your past, present, and future for the highest good.

CONCLUSION

Pendulum dowsing is special because it blends simplicity with profound potential, making it accessible to anyone interested in spiritual growth, self-discovery, and healing. It provides a direct, versatile, and empowering way to connect with your inner wisdom and the energies around you, making it a valuable tool for self healing and enhancing your spiritual practice.

748

HOW TO RECEIVE A PENDULUM ATTUNEMENT!

Pendulum attunement is a process of energetically aligning and empowering your pendulum to enhance its accuracy, sensitivity, and connection to your intuitive guidance. This attunement can help synchronize the pendulum with your energy field and intentions, allowing it to serve as a more effective tool for dowsing, healing, and spiritual work.

CHOOSE THE RIGHT PENDULUM:

- Select a pendulum that feels right for you. It can be made of metal, crystal, wood, or any material that resonates with you.

- Ensure the pendulum is cleansed and free of any residual or negative energies. You can cleanse it by holding it under running water, smudging it with sage, placing it in sunlight or moonlight, or using your preferred cleansing method.

CREATE A SACRED SPACE:

- Find a quiet, comfortable space where you won't be disturbed. This can be a dedicated meditation area or any place where you feel safe and calm.

- Arrange any items that help you feel connected to your spiritual practice, such as candles, crystals, or incense. You may also want to play calming music or nature sounds to enhance the atmosphere.

GROUND AND CENTER YOURSELF:

- Sit or stand comfortably and take several deep breaths to ground and center your energy. Imagine roots extending from your feet deep into the earth, anchoring you firmly in place.

- Visualize a beam of light coming from above, connecting you to the universe or your higher self. Feel this light entering your crown, filling your body, and surrounding you with a protective, loving energy.

SET YOUR INTENTION FOR ATTUNEMENT:

- Hold your pendulum in your dominant hand and place it over your heart or in front of you. Close your eyes and set a clear intention for the attunement process.

- You might say silently or out loud: "I intend to attune this pendulum to my highest vibration, so it may serve as a clear, accurate, and effective tool for guidance, healing, and connection to my inner wisdom."

INVOKE GUIDANCE AND SUPPORT:

- Call upon your spiritual guides, angels, ancestors, or any higher power you resonate with to assist in the attunement process. Ask for their guidance, protection, and blessings.

- You can say something like: "I invite my spirit guides, angels, and higher self to support me in attuning this pendulum to its highest potential, aligning it with my truth, light, and purpose."

VISUALIZE THE ATTUNEMENT PROCESS:

- Visualize a beam of pure, white or golden light coming from above, flowing into your pendulum. Imagine this light filling the pendulum, cleansing it of any unwanted energies, and charging it with positive, healing vibrations.

- See the light growing brighter, surrounding the pendulum, and connecting it with your energy field. Feel this connection becoming stronger, allowing the pendulum to resonate with your personal energy and intentions.

HOLD THE PENDULUM OVER EACH CHAKRA:

- Slowly move the pendulum over each of your chakras, starting from the root chakra and moving up to the crown chakra. Allow the pendulum to spin or move naturally over each energy center.

- As you do this, visualize the energy from each chakra aligning with the pendulum, creating a strong energetic bond between the pendulum and your body. Feel the pendulum attuning to your unique vibrational frequency.

PROGRAM THE PENDULUM WITH SPECIFIC INTENTIONS:

- Once the attunement is complete, program the pendulum with specific intentions or commands that align with your goals. For example, you might say:

- "I program this pendulum to provide me with accurate guidance for my highest good," or "I charge this pendulum to help me clear negative energies and promote healing."

- You can also specify that the pendulum is attuned for a particular purpose, such as dowsing, energy healing, manifestation, or spiritual communication.

TEST YOUR ATTUNEMENT:

- After the attunement, test your pendulum by asking it simple questions to which you already know the answers. Observe its movements to ensure it is responding accurately and consistently.

- If the responses feel off or unclear, repeat the attunement process, focusing on areas where you feel there may be blockages or misalignments.

EXPRESS GRATITUDE AND CLOSE THE ATTUNEMENT:

- Once you feel the attunement is complete and the pendulum is fully aligned with your energy, express gratitude to your guides, angels, or higher self for their support and guidance.

- You might say: "Thank you for attuning this pendulum to my highest vibration. I am grateful for this connection and the wisdom it brings."

ADDITIONAL TIPS FOR PENDULUM ATTUNEMENT

- ## REGULARLY RE-ATTUNE YOUR PENDULUM:

  Just as you cleanse your pendulum regularly, you may also wish to re-attune it from time to time, especially if you feel its energy is not as strong or clear as it should be.

- ## PERSONALIZE YOUR ATTUNEMENT PROCESS:

  Feel free to modify the steps to suit your spiritual beliefs and practices. You can add prayers, affirmations, or rituals that feel right for you.

- ## TRUST YOUR INTUITION:

  The most crucial aspect of attunement is trusting your intuition. If you feel guided to do something differently during the attunement process, follow that guidance.

By attuning your pendulum, you create a stronger, more harmonious connection between the tool and your inner guidance, allowing for clearer communication, effective dowsing, and enhanced spiritual practice.

PENDULUM MOVEMENTS AND THEIR MEANINGS

When using a pendulum for dowsing, the movements of the pendulum - such as swinging clockwise, counterclockwise (anticlockwise), or in a "flower" pattern - are believed to convey specific meanings or responses from your subconscious mind, higher self, or spiritual guides. Here is what each of these common pendulum movements generally signifies:

CLOCKWISE MOVEMENT

- **POSITIVE RESPONSE:**

  A clockwise (rightward) circular motion is often interpreted as a "Yes" or positive answer. It may also indicate that the energy around the question or situation is clear, balanced, and aligned.

- **CONFIRMATION AND AFFIRMATION:**

  A clockwise movement can signify confirmation or affirmation, indicating that the energy is moving in the right direction or that the situation is favorable.

- **CLEARING OR HEALING:**

  In energy work or healing contexts, a clockwise movement can also indicate that the pendulum is actively clearing or energizing an area, such as balancing chakras or releasing blockages.

COUNTERCLOCKWISE (ANTICLOCKWISE) MOVEMENT

- ### NEGATIVE RESPONSE:

  A counterclockwise (leftward) circular motion is often interpreted as a "No" or negative answer. It may indicate resistance, imbalance, or that the energy around the question or situation is not aligned or in harmony.

- ### RELEASING OR CLEARING BLOCKAGES:

  In healing contexts, a counterclockwise movement can signify the release of negative energies, clearing blockages, or purging unwanted emotions or patterns. It may indicate that the pendulum is removing or dispelling something that no longer serves your highest good.

- ### WARNING OR CAUTION:

  This movement can also serve as a warning or indication to proceed with caution, especially when considering decisions or actions.

FLOWER PATTERN MOVEMENT

- ## BALANCED AND HARMONIOUS ENERGY:

  A "flower" pattern, where the pendulum moves in a combination of circular and elliptical motions, often represents balanced, harmonious, or neutral energy. This movement may suggest that multiple aspects of a situation are coming together in a balanced way, or that there is a mix of energies involved.

- ## INTEGRATION AND SYNTHESIS:

  The flower pattern can indicate that energies are integrating or synthesizing, bringing different elements into alignment. This is often seen in healing or spiritual work where multiple layers or aspects of a situation are being addressed simultaneously.

- ## SIGN OF EXPANSION OR EVOLUTION:

  A flower pattern can symbolize growth, expansion, or evolution, suggesting that the situation is unfolding in a dynamic, fluid, and positive manner. It might also indicate spiritual or personal development and the blossoming of new opportunities.

BACK AND FORTH (VERTICAL OR HORIZONTAL):

- A straight back-and-forth motion, either vertically or horizontally, is often used to indicate "Yes" (up and down) or "No" (side to side), depending on how you have programmed your pendulum to respond.

DIAGONAL MOVEMENT:

- A diagonal movement may represent uncertainty, a need for more clarity, or that additional information is needed before a clear response can be given.

INTERPRETING PENDULUM MOVEMENTS

The meanings of pendulum movements can vary based on how you have programmed your pendulum and your personal intuition or experience. To accurately interpret your pendulum's movements:

- **PROGRAM YOUR PENDULUM:**

  Establish a set of consistent meanings for different movements. For example, you might decide that vertical movement means "Yes" and horizontal movement means "No." Test these meanings by asking simple questions to which you already know the answers.

- **TRUST YOUR INTUITION:**

  Pay attention to how you feel when the pendulum moves in certain ways. Your intuition can provide additional insight or context that might not be immediately obvious from the pendulum's movement alone.

- **PRACTICE REGULARLY:**

  The more you practice, the more familiar you will become with the pendulum's unique responses and movements. Consistency and regular practice will help you develop a deeper connection with your pendulum.

By understanding the meanings of these movements, you can use your pendulum more effectively for dowsing, healing, and spiritual guidance, enhancing your ability to connect with your inner wisdom and the energies around you.

HOW TO USE A PENDULUM FOR HEALING!

Pendulum healing is a powerful technique that uses the pendulum as a tool to detect, clear, and balance energetic disturbances in the body, mind, and spirit. It is based on the principle that everything is energy and that imbalances or blockages in this energy can manifest as physical, emotional, or spiritual issues. By using a pendulum, you can tap into your intuitive guidance and the energy field to facilitate healing. Here are some key ways to use a pendulum for healing:

DETECTING AND BALANCING ENERGY IMBALANCES

- **SCANNING THE AURA AND CHAKRAS:**

  The pendulum can be used to scan a person's aura or energy field to detect areas of imbalance or blockages. Hold the pendulum over each chakra or area of the body and observe its movement. If the pendulum moves erratically, spins counterclockwise, or stops, it may indicate an energy blockage or imbalance.

- **BALANCING CHAKRAS:**

  Once an imbalance is detected, you can use the pendulum to help balance the chakras. Hold the pendulum over each chakra and allow it to move naturally. A clockwise movement typically indicates that energy is being balanced and cleared, while a counterclockwise movement may suggest the release of stagnant or negative energy. Continue until the pendulum's movement becomes steady or clockwise, indicating the energy is balanced.

CLEARING NEGATIVE ENERGIES AND BLOCKAGES

- **REMOVING EMOTIONAL BLOCKAGES:**

  Pendulum healing can help clear emotional blockages such as fear, anger, sadness, or anxiety. You can ask the pendulum to show you where these blockages are located in the body or energy field. Once identified, use the pendulum to clear these energies by focusing on the area and intending that the negative emotions are released and transmuted into positive energy.

- **CLEARING PAST TRAUMA OR NEGATIVE INFLUENCES:**

  Pendulum healing can also help release energy from past traumas, karmic influences, or negative experiences that may be affecting your current state. You can ask the pendulum specific questions to identify the source of these influences and then use it to energetically clear them.

ENHANCING ENERGY FLOW AND VITALITY

- **BOOSTING ENERGY LEVELS:**

  The pendulum can help boost your overall energy levels by aligning and enhancing the flow of energy throughout your body. You can ask the pendulum to channel healing energy into specific areas where you feel depleted or fatigued. The pendulum's movement may change as it directs energy into these areas.

- **IMPROVING PHYSICAL HEALTH:**

  Use the pendulum to focus on specific physical health issues. You can ask questions such as "Is there an energy blockage affecting my [specific organ or body part]?" or "What does my body need for optimal health?" The pendulum can help identify areas of concern and direct energy for healing.

RELEASING NEGATIVE BELIEFS AND PATTERNS

- **IDENTIFYING LIMITING BELIEFS:**

  Pendulum healing can help uncover limiting beliefs or negative thought patterns that may be impacting your emotional or spiritual well-being. You can ask the pendulum questions to identify these beliefs, such as "Do I have a belief that is limiting my ability to feel confident?" Once identified, use the pendulum to clear these beliefs by focusing on releasing them and replacing them with positive affirmations.

- **TRANSFORMING NEGATIVE PATTERNS:**

  After identifying negative beliefs, the pendulum can be used to energetically shift or transform these patterns. You can use the pendulum to focus on the energy surrounding these beliefs and command it to transmute them into positive, supportive patterns.

ACCESSING PAST LIFE HEALING

- ## EXPLORING PAST LIFE ISSUES:

  Pendulum dowsing can help explore and heal
  past life issues that may be influencing your
  current life. You can ask the pendulum to identify
  past life events, traumas, or unresolved issues
  that are affecting you now. Once identified, use
  the pendulum to clear any negative energies or
  influences from these past lives.

- ## HEALING KARMIC PATTERNS:

  The pendulum can assist in healing karmic
  patterns or unresolved lessons from past lives.
  Focus on the specific karmic issue you wish to
  address, and use the pendulum to release any
  lingering energies, beliefs, or attachments from
  those past experiences.

ENHANCING EMOTIONAL HEALING

- **RELEASING EMOTIONAL PAIN:**

  The pendulum can be used to release emotional pain or trauma that may be held in the body or energy field. You can ask the pendulum to help identify the location of the emotional pain and then use it to energetically release or transmute the pain into healing energy.

- **PROMOTING EMOTIONAL BALANCE:**

  By using the pendulum to balance the energy centers, you can promote emotional balance and harmony. This can help alleviate symptoms of stress, anxiety, depression, or emotional overwhelm, bringing a sense of calm and peace.

SUPPORTING SPIRITUAL GROWTH

- **ENHANCING INTUITION AND SPIRITUAL CONNECTION**:

  Pendulum healing can enhance your intuitive abilities and strengthen your connection to your higher self, spiritual guides, or divine energy. Use the pendulum to ask questions that guide your spiritual journey, help you understand your life purpose, or provide insights into your spiritual growth.

- **CLEARING SPIRITUAL BLOCKAGES:**

  If you feel spiritually stuck or disconnected, the pendulum can help identify and clear any blockages that may be hindering your spiritual progress. Ask the pendulum to show you where these blockages are and use it to energetically clear them.

MANIFESTATION AND GOAL SETTING

- ## ALIGNING WITH DESIRES:

  The pendulum can help align your energy with
  your desires or goals by clearing any
  subconscious blocks or resistance that may be
  preventing manifestation. You can ask the
  pendulum specific questions to identify these
  blocks and use it to energetically remove them.

- ## EMPOWERING AFFIRMATIONS:

  Use the pendulum to reinforce positive
  affirmations and intentions by focusing on your
  desired outcomes and allowing the pendulum to
  move in alignment with your intention. This can
  strengthen the energetic vibration of your
  affirmations and enhance their manifestation
  potential.

HOW TO PERFORM PENDULUM HEALING!

PREPARE THE PENDULUM:

- Cleanse your pendulum by holding it under running water, smudging it with sage, placing it in sunlight or moonlight, or using your preferred method.

- Set a clear intention for the healing session. You might say, "I intend to use this pendulum for the highest good, to bring healing, balance, and positive energy."

CREATE A SACRED SPACE:

- Find a quiet, comfortable space where you won't be disturbed. You can light a candle, burn incense, or play calming music to create a peaceful atmosphere.

GROUND AND CENTER YOURSELF:

- Take a few deep breaths to center yourself. Imagine roots extending from your feet into the earth, grounding you. Visualize a beam of light connecting you to the universe or your higher self.

ASK FOR GUIDANCE AND PROTECTION:

- Call upon your spiritual guides, angels, or any higher power you resonate with to assist and protect you during the healing session.

IDENTIFY THE HEALING FOCUS:

- Hold the pendulum over your body, a chakra, or a specific area needing healing. Ask specific questions to identify blockages, imbalances, or areas that require attention.

OBSERVE THE PENDULUM'S MOVEMENTS:

- Allow the pendulum to move naturally and observe its direction, speed, and pattern. Interpret the movement to determine if energy is being released, cleared, or balanced.

DIRECT HEALING ENERGY:

- Focus your intention on directing healing energy through the pendulum. Imagine a light beam or energy flow from the universe, through your body, into the pendulum, and into the area needing healing.

CLOSE THE SESSION:

- Once you feel the healing is complete, thank your guides and the universe for their assistance. Cleanse the pendulum again if needed, and take a few moments to ground yourself by taking deep breaths

PENDULUM DOWSING TECHNIQUES:

Pendulum dowsing is an ancient technique used to tap into your subconscious mind and connect with your intuition to gain insights, answer questions, and perform healing. By using a pendulum - a small weighted object suspended on a chain or string - you can communicate with your inner guidance and access deeper layers of awareness.

ASKING CLEAR QUESTIONS:

- Frame your questions in a way that can be answered with "Yes," "No," or "Maybe." Clear, specific questions yield the most accurate answers.

- Avoid vague or complex questions. Instead of asking, "What should I do about my career?" try "Is it beneficial for me to pursue this specific job opportunity?"

USING CHARTS FOR DOWSING:

- Pendulum charts are visual aids that help you determine answers or directions. They can range from simple "Yes/No" charts to more complex ones with multiple options or scales.

- Hold your pendulum over the chart and ask your question. Allow the pendulum to guide you to the correct section of the chart. This is especially useful for identifying specific issues, healing sessions, or areas of focus.

CLEARING ENERGY BLOCKS:

- If you sense energetic blockages, ask your pendulum to identify them. You might ask, "Is there an energy block in my [area of life]?" If the answer is "Yes," proceed to ask more specific questions to locate and understand the blockage.

- Use the pendulum to clear the blockage by affirming, "I release this energy block with love and light," while visualizing the pendulum clearing the energy.

PROGRAMMING YOUR PENDULUM:

- You can program your pendulum to work with specific intentions or purposes. For example, before starting a session, you might say, "I program this pendulum to reveal the most beneficial information for my highest good."

- Programming helps align the pendulum with your purpose and creates a focused channel for information.

USING DOWSING COMMANDS FOR HEALING:

- Dowsing commands are specific instructions you give to your pendulum to initiate healing. For example, you might say, "Clear all negative energy from my heart chakra" while holding the pendulum over your heart.

- Commands can be used to release, transmute, or balance energies. Combine them with visualizations to amplify their effectiveness.

ACCESSING SUBCONSCIOUS WISDOM:

- Pendulum dowsing can help you tap into the wisdom of your subconscious mind. You can ask questions like, "What belief is holding me back from success?" or "What is my subconscious fear regarding this situation?"

- The pendulum's movements can help you identify hidden fears, limiting beliefs, or past traumas that need healing.

USING DOWSING FOR MANIFESTATION:

- You can use pendulum dowsing to align your energy with your goals. Ask, "Am I aligned with the energy of abundance?" or "What do I need to do to manifest [desired outcome]?"

- Use the pendulum to reinforce positive affirmations and commands, such as, "I attract abundance effortlessly" or "I am open to receiving love and joy."

By integrating these pendulum dowsing techniques into your daily practice, you can effectively connect with your inner guidance, clear energetic blockages, and manifest your highest good.

SAFETY INSTRUCTIONS

SET CLEAR INTENTIONS:

- Before starting any dowsing session, set a clear intention for what you want to achieve. State that you are working for the highest good and seek only positive, beneficial outcomes.

- You might say, "I intend to receive guidance that is accurate, safe, and for my highest good and the highest good of all involved."

GROUND AND PROTECT YOUR ENERGY:

- Ensure you are grounded and centered before beginning a session. Grounding techniques include deep breathing, visualization, or imagining roots extending from your feet into the earth.

- Visualize a protective shield of light surrounding you to safeguard your energy. You can ask your guides, angels, or a higher power to provide protection during the session.

MAINTAIN A NEUTRAL STATE OF MIND:

- Approach dowsing with neutrality. Do not let emotions, desires, or preconceived notions influence your questions or interpretation of the results.

- Avoid dowsing when you are feeling anxious, angry, or emotionally charged, as this can distort the accuracy of the responses.

KEEP QUESTIONS FOCUSED AND SPECIFIC:

- Ask clear, concise questions that can be answered with "Yes," "No," or "Maybe." Vague or open-ended questions may lead to ambiguous or misleading answers.

- Avoid repetitive questioning about the same issue in a short time frame, as it may create confusion and reduce the reliability of the results.

RESPECT YOUR PHYSICAL AND EMOTIONAL LIMITS:

- If you feel tired, dizzy, or unwell during a dowsing session, stop immediately. Take breaks and ensure you are hydrated and comfortable.

- Trust your intuition if you feel uneasy or if something doesn't feel right. End the session and ground yourself.

CLEAR AND CLEANSE YOUR PENDULUM REGULARLY:

- Cleanse your pendulum after each session to remove any negative or unwanted energy it may have picked up. Methods include running it under cool water, placing it in sunlight or moonlight, or using smoke from sage or incense.

- Hold the pendulum in your hand and set the intention to clear any energy that doesn't serve you or the highest good.

ETHICAL GUIDELINES

AVOID DOWSING FOR OTHERS WITHOUT CONSENT:

- Do not use your pendulum to ask questions about other people without their permission. This respects their privacy and free will.

- If someone asks you to dowse on their behalf, ensure they are fully aware of the process, and ask for their consent to proceed.

SEEK THE HIGHEST GOOD:

- Always dowse with the intention to serve the highest good of yourself and others. Avoid using the pendulum for harmful or selfish purposes.

- Remember that the purpose of dowsing is to gain insight, healing, and personal growth—not to control or manipulate outcomes or others.

RESPECT FREE WILL:

- Respect the free will of others by not dowsing for them without their explicit consent.

- Understand that everyone has the right to make their own choices and decisions. Your role as a dowser is not to impose your findings on others but to offer guidance if requested.

USE FOR POSITIVE PURPOSES:

- Use pendulum dowsing for positive, constructive, and ethical purposes only. Examples include personal healing, gaining insight, clearing energy, and manifesting positive outcomes.

- Avoid using dowsing to interfere in others' lives, uncover secrets, or perform harmful actions.

INTERPRET RESPONSIBLY:

- Be mindful when interpreting pendulum responses. Understand that dowsing is not an exact science; it relies heavily on intuition and subconscious signals.

- Don't make critical life decisions solely based on dowsing results. Consider using dowsing as one of many tools for decision-making, alongside rational thought, research, and professional advice.

AVOID PREDICTING THE FUTURE:

- Refrain from using dowsing as a means to predict the future with certainty. The future is fluid and influenced by countless variables, including free will and changing circumstances.

- Instead, use dowsing to gain insight into present conditions, energy patterns, or the potential consequences of different choices.

RESPECT CONFIDENTIALITY:

- If you dowse for others, maintain confidentiality and respect their privacy. Do not share their information, questions, or results without their permission.

- Be transparent with anyone you are dowsing for about your process, the limitations of dowsing, and any possible outcomes.

ACKNOWLEDGE LIMITATIONS:

- Understand and acknowledge the limitations of dowsing. It is a spiritual and intuitive tool, not a substitute for medical, legal, or professional advice.

- Encourage others to seek appropriate professional help when needed, and use dowsing as a complementary practice.

STAY OPEN-MINDED AND HUMBLE:

- Stay open-minded and humble about the information received. Acknowledge that dowsing may not always provide clear answers or that your interpretation might not always be correct.

- Recognize that dowsing is a practice that involves growth, learning, and continuous self-improvement.

TIPS FOR EFFECTIVE PENDULUM HEALING

- **PRACTICE REGULARLY:**

  The more you use your pendulum for healing, the more effective it becomes as you develop a deeper connection with it.

- **STAY OPEN AND TRUSTING:**

  While the pendulum provides guidance, always listen to your inner voice. The pendulum is a tool to access your intuition, not a replacement for it.

- **STAY NEUTRAL:**

  Approach dowsing with an open mind and avoid projecting your desires or expectations onto the pendulum.

- **BE GROUNDED AND CENTERED:**

  Make sure you are calm, grounded, and in a balanced state of mind to ensure accurate results.

- **USE AFFIRMATIONS:**

  Pair pendulum healing with affirmations to reinforce positive energy and intention.

PART 1:

LIFE HEALING

1.

TRAUMATIC EVENTS WORKSHEETS

Traumatic events are deeply distressing or disturbing experiences that can overwhelm an individual's ability to cope. These events may involve a threat to life or safety, leaving a lasting impact on one's mental and emotional well-being. Trauma can manifest in various forms, such as accidents, natural disasters, or violence, often leading to long-term psychological effects like anxiety, depression, or PTSD. Healing from trauma requires time, support, and, often, therapeutic intervention to rebuild a sense of safety and restore emotional balance.

HEALING SESSION NO: 1
TRAUMATIC EVENT

INTENT SETTING:

- "I intend to clear, release, transmute, and heal all negative energies, emotions, and patterns associated with the traumatic event [briefly describe the event or hold it in your mind]. I will go back to the moment this trauma occurred to clear and heal it at its source. I invite pure love, light, and healing to transform this energy into a source of strength and wisdom, and to secure my future from similar experiences."

INITIAL CLEARING:

- "I command to clear, release, and transmute all negative energy, emotions, and patterns associated with this event across all time, space, dimensions, and lifetimes. Clear any residual effects on my physical, emotional, mental, and spiritual bodies."

GOING BACK IN TIME:

- "I now go back in time to the exact moment when this traumatic event occurred. I enter the scene as an observer, with the intention to clear and heal the energy from its source."

Visualize yourself in the moment the trauma occurred. See the surroundings, feel the energy, and observe the emotions involved.

DEEP CLEARING AND HEALING AT THE SOURCE:

- "I command to clear and release all negative energies, emotions, and patterns that were created or amplified by this event. Clear all energies of shock, fear, pain, and distress that may have been stored in my body and aura."

- "I command to release all attachments, cords, and contracts connected to this event that no longer serve my highest good. I sever and dissolve all negative energetic ties to this event and any people involved."

- "I command to transmute the energy of this traumatic event into pure love and light. I send healing energy to all involved, including myself. I fill this moment with the energies of safety, peace, and understanding, healing it completely at its source."*

Visualize a bright, healing light enveloping the scene, transforming all negativity into love and light.

HEALING THE EMOTIONAL AND PHYSICAL IMPACT:

- "I command to heal and soothe all emotional and physical wounds caused by this event. I invite the energy of unconditional love to fill my entire being, healing any feelings of fear, sadness, anger, guilt, or pain that may have arisen from this experience."

Visualize your entire being filling with a warm, loving light that radiates throughout your body, healing all aspects of your being.

RELEASING LIMITING BELIEFS AND PATTERNS:

- "I command to identify and release any limiting beliefs or patterns that were created or reinforced by this event. I release the belief that [insert specific belief related to the event, e.g., 'I am not safe,' 'I am powerless,' etc.]. I replace these with empowering beliefs aligned with my highest good."

Allow the pendulum to move and feel the old beliefs dissolving, replaced by new, empowering ones.

HARMONIZATION AND INTEGRATION:

- "I command to harmonize and integrate the positive lessons and growth from this event into the timeline of my life. I integrate this healed energy into my present self, ensuring that I am stronger, wiser, and more resilient."

Allow the pendulum to move and feel the energy shifting within you.

SECURING THE FUTURE:

- "I command to secure my future from experiencing similar traumatic events. I establish a protective shield around my energy field, allowing only positive, empowering experiences to come into my life. I program this shield to deflect any energies or situations that do not serve my highest good."

Visualize a protective shield of light surrounding you, strong and impenetrable, yet flexible enough to allow in only positive energy.

- "I command to align my future experiences with my highest potential and my soul's purpose. I attract only those situations, people, and opportunities that support my growth, happiness, and well-being."

Visualize your future filled with positive, fulfilling experiences that align with your highest self.

SEALING THE HEALING:

- "I command to seal all the healing work done during this session. I seal this healing in pure love, light, and divine protection, ensuring that it is permanent and irrevocable. No outside force or energy can undo or disturb the healing that has taken place."

Visualize a powerful, golden light enveloping the entire healing process, locking in the positive changes and sealing them completely.

- "I command to seal my energy field, protecting it from any lower vibrations, entities, or influences. This seal is fortified with divine protection and will only allow in energies that align with my highest good."

Imagine your energy field being encased in a protective layer of light, impenetrable to anything that doesn't serve your highest good.

PENDULUM QUESTIONS:

After completing the commands, use your pendulum to ask the following questions to ensure the session's effectiveness and uncover any remaining areas that may need attention:

1. Has all negative energy associated with this event been fully cleared?

2. Are there any lingering emotions or patterns that still need to be addressed?

3. Is there any remaining energy from this event affecting my present life?

4. Has the energy of this event been fully transmuted into love and light?

5. Is the healing and transformation from this session fully integrated into my being?

6. Is my future now fully protected from similar traumatic events?

7. Has the healing work from this session been permanently sealed?

8. Is my energy field fully sealed and protected?

9. Are there any additional steps I need to take to reinforce the healing?

10. Is there anything else I need to know or do regarding this event?

Use your pendulum to receive answers to each question, and if any issues remain, repeat the relevant clearing or healing commands as needed.

AFFIRMATION:

Close the session by repeating the following affirmation:

- "I am free from the traumatic energy of the past. I have healed this event at its source and transmuted it into love and light. I am protected, and my future is filled with positive, empowering experiences. The healing work done today is sealed and permanent. I move forward with strength, wisdom, and peace."

HEALING SESSION NO: 2

PAST LIFE TRAUMA

SETTING THE INTENTION

- "Set the intention to uncover, clear, and heal any past life trauma that is affecting my current life. Align this session with the highest good, under the guidance of divine wisdom and protection."

- "Is this intention clearly set and aligned with my highest good?"

GROUNDING AND PROTECTION:

- "Ground me deeply to the Earth, anchoring my energy firmly in the present moment."

- "Surround me with a protective shield of divine white light, impenetrable by any negative or lower energies."

- "Strengthen my energetic boundaries, allowing only pure love and light to enter."

- "Am I fully grounded and protected?"

CONNECTING TO HIGHER GUIDANCE

- "Connect me to my Higher Self, spirit guides, and all beings of pure love and light who are here to assist me in this healing."

- "Ensure that I receive clear and accurate guidance throughout this session, free from interference."

- "Am I connected to my Higher Self and divine guidance for this healing session?"

If no,

- "Connect me now to my Higher Self and divine guidance, ensuring a clear and pure connection."

IDENTIFYING THE PAST LIFE TRAUMA

- "Reveal to me any past life traumas that are currently impacting my life. Show me the most significant trauma that needs healing now."

- "Bring forth the details of this trauma in a way that is safe and understandable for me."

- "Clear any fear or resistance to uncovering this trauma, allowing me to see it clearly and objectively."

- "Is there a specific past life trauma that is affecting my current life?"

If yes, continue asking:

- "Is this trauma related to relationships?"

- "Is this trauma related to health?"

- "Is this trauma related to career?"

- "Is this trauma related to financial issues?"

- "Is this trauma related to emotional well-being?"

- Is there more than one trauma affecting my current life?"

TIME-TRAVEL VISUALIZATION

- "Guide me safely through time to the specific lifetime where this trauma originated."

- "Create a safe and supportive environment as I witness the events and emotions tied to this trauma."

Visualize yourself traveling back through lifetimes. When you reach the source:

- "Am I in the correct lifetime where this trauma began?"

- "Show me the events and emotions connected to this trauma in a way that I can understand and heal."

- "Ensure that I remain detached and protected as I observe this past life, absorbing only what is necessary for healing."

CLEARING THE TRAUMA

- "Clear, release, and transmute all negative energy, emotions, and patterns associated with this past life trauma into pure love and light."

- "Dissolve any energetic cords, attachments, or vows connected to this trauma that no longer serve my highest good."

- "Release all karmic debt and soul contracts linked to this trauma, allowing complete freedom and resolution."

- "Erase all memories, imprints, and energetic residues from this trauma across all dimensions, timelines, and realities."

- "Has this trauma been fully cleared?"

If not,

- "Clear any remaining residue or resistance related to this trauma."

- "Transmute any negative energy connected to this trauma into pure love and light, ensuring it no longer affects me."

HEALING THE PAST LIFE

- "Infuse this past life with healing light, bringing resolution, forgiveness, and peace to all involved."

- "Heal all wounds, physical, emotional, and spiritual, that were created as a result of this trauma."

- "Restore balance and harmony to this past life, ensuring that all energies are transmuted to love and light."

- "Integrate this healing into my soul's blueprint, ensuring it benefits my current life."

Visualize the past life being surrounded by healing light.

- "Is this past life fully healed?"

- "Integrate the healing from this past life into my present life with ease and grace."

SECURING THE FUTURE

- "Seal this healing so that the effects are permanent and complete across all lifetimes."

- "Protect my future from any lingering effects of this past trauma, ensuring I am free from its influence now and forever."

- "Strengthen the positive energy in my life, replacing the space once held by the trauma with love, abundance, and joy."

- "Is my future fully secure from this past trauma?"

HARMONIZING THE PRESENT

- "Harmonize all aspects of my current life with this healing, aligning my mind, body, and spirit with the highest frequencies of love and light."

- "Balance my energy fields, chakras, and auric layers, ensuring they reflect the healing and freedom I have received."

- "Ensure that this healing manifests as positive changes in my life, enhancing my overall well-being and happiness."

- "Is my present life fully harmonized with this healing?"

- "Strengthen this harmony, allowing peace, joy, and well-being to flow into all areas of my life."

GRATITUDE AND CLOSING:

- "Seal this healing with gratitude, love, and light, ensuring that all work done in this session is protected and complete."

- "Close this session, returning all energies to their rightful place, and grounding me fully back in the present moment."

- "Thank all guides, angels, and higher beings who assisted in this session. Express deep gratitude for the healing received."

- "Is this session fully closed and complete?"

INTEGRATION

- "Assist in fully integrating this healing into every aspect of my life, ensuring ongoing benefits and well-being."

- "Allow my body, mind, and spirit to rest and rejuvenate as I integrate the healing from this session."

- "Support the manifestation of this healing into my daily life, allowing me to experience the full benefits with ease."

- "Fortify this security with pure love and light, ensuring ongoing protection and freedom."

HEALING SESSION NO: 3
TRAUMA AT BIRTH

ESTABLISH CONNECTION

- "I now connect with my highest self, my guides, the divine source of all healing energy, and any beings of pure light who can assist in this healing. I ask for guidance, protection, and clarity throughout this session. I am safe, supported, and surrounded by pure love and light."

PENDULUM QUESTIONS

- "Am I fully connected to my highest self and guides?"

- "Is my connection with the divine source of healing energy clear and strong?"

- "Is there anything else I need to do to ensure a strong connection for this session?"

If the pendulum swings positively to all questions, continue to the next step. If the pendulum swings negatively to any question, repeat the connection command and ask again until the pendulum confirms readiness.

IDENTIFY THE TRAUMA

- "I now ask to be shown the exact moment of my birth where any trauma was imprinted upon my being. I invite this memory to surface in a way that is gentle, supportive, and safe for my healing."

PENDULUM QUESTIONS:

- "Has the moment of birth trauma been identified?"

- "Was the trauma related to physical pain?"

- "Was the trauma related to emotional distress?"

- "Was the trauma related to fear or anxiety?"

- "Are there any other factors contributing to this trauma?"

If the pendulum swings positively to the first question, proceed to the next step. If the pendulum swings negatively, allow more time for the information to surface and ask again.

CLEAR AND RELEASE THE TRAUMA:

- "I now command that all trauma, pain, fear, and distress associated with my birth be fully cleared, released, and transmuted into pure love and light. I release all negative imprints, beliefs, and patterns formed during my birth, sending them into the light for complete healing."

- "I command that any residual energy, emotions, or memories from this trauma be completely dissolved, never to return. I now fill the space left by this release with unconditional love, peace, and harmony."

- I command that all physical imprints of this trauma be erased from my cellular memory. My body is now free from any influence of this birth trauma."

- "I command that all emotional wounds caused by this trauma be healed and transmuted into pure love. I release all emotional pain associated with my birth, allowing only love and peace to remain."

- "I command that all mental patterns formed as a result of this trauma be dissolved and replaced with thoughts of love, safety, and empowerment. My mind is now clear and aligned with my highest good."

PENDULUM QUESTIONS:

- "Has the birth trauma been fully cleared and released?"

- "Are there any hidden or subconscious aspects of this trauma that need to be addressed?"

- "Is there any energy from this trauma still lingering in my physical body?"

- "Is there any energy from this trauma still affecting my emotional body?"

- "Is there any energy from this trauma still influencing my mental body?

HEAL AND TRANSFORM

- "I now command that my entire being - body, mind, and spirit - be fully healed from the effects of this birth trauma. I invite the energy of divine love and healing to fill every cell of my body, restoring perfect health, balance, and wholeness."

- "I command that any wounds, scars, or damage from this trauma be completely healed, leaving no trace behind. I am reborn in perfect love and light."

- "I command that any energetic blockages caused by this trauma be fully dissolved, allowing my energy to flow freely and harmoniously throughout my entire being."

- "I command that my energy field be fully restored, repaired, and strengthened. Any tears, holes, or weaknesses caused by this trauma are now mended and fortified with divine love and light."

- "I command that my nervous system be fully balanced and calmed, releasing any tension or stress that may have resulted from this trauma. I am now at peace, calm, and centered."

- "I command that my heart be fully opened to receiving and giving love, free from any fear or pain associated with my birth. My heart is now healed and overflowing with love and joy."

PENDULUM QUESTIONS:

- "Has the healing and transformation been fully completed?"

- "Is my physical body now fully healed from this trauma?"

- "Is my emotional body now fully healed from this trauma?"

- "Is my mental body now fully healed from this trauma?"

- "Is my energy field fully restored and balanced?"

- "Are there any other aspects of my being that require healing?"

If the pendulum swings positively to the first question and negatively to the others, continue to the next step. If the pendulum swings positively to any of the follow-up questions, repeat the healing commands until the pendulum confirms completion.

SECURE THE FUTURE

- "I now command that all future experiences be free from the influence of this birth trauma. I secure my future with the energy of pure love, joy, and ease. My life is filled with positive, nurturing experiences that support my highest good."

- "I command that my future be aligned with my true purpose, mission, and highest potential, free from any past traumas. I am now fully empowered to live a life of peace, happiness, and fulfillment."

- "I command that any residual effects of this trauma be fully neutralized and transmuted, ensuring they cannot influence my future in any way."

- "I command that all aspects of my life—relationships, health, career, and personal growth—be fully protected and aligned with my highest good, free from any lingering effects of this trauma."

- "I command that my future self be empowered with strength, confidence, and resilience, ensuring that I am fully equipped to handle any challenges with grace and ease."

PENDULUM QUESTIONS:

- "Is my future now secure and free from the influence of past birth trauma?"

- "Are there any specific areas of my life that still need attention to secure my future?"

- "Is there anything else I need to do to fully secure my future?"

If the pendulum swings positively to the first question and negatively to the others, move to the closing. If the pendulum swings positively to any of the follow-up questions, repeat the securing commands as needed.

CLOSING THE SESSION

- "I now disconnect from any energies, guides, or beings I connected with during this session. I am fully grounded, centered, and at peace. I thank all who assisted in this healing process. I am now free from the effects of any birth trauma, and I step forward into my life with confidence, joy, and love."

- "I command that any residual energy from this session be fully integrated into my being in a harmonious and balanced way. I am now aligned with my highest good, and all aspects of my life reflect this alignment."

PENDULUM QUESTIONS:

- "Is the session now complete?"

- "Have all connections been fully and safely closed?"

- "Am I fully grounded and centered?"

If the pendulum swings positively to all questions, your session is complete. If the pendulum swings negatively to any question, take a moment to breathe deeply and repeat the closing command until the pendulum confirms closure.

HEALING SESSION NO: 4
TRAUMATIC MEMORIES

Hold your pendulum in your dominant hand, and keep your focus on the intention of healing traumatic memories.

ESTABLISH CONNECTION:

- "I now connect with my highest self, my guides, the divine source of all healing energy, and any beings of pure light who can assist in this healing. I ask for guidance, protection, and clarity throughout this session. I am safe, supported, and surrounded by pure love and light."

PENDULUM QUESTIONS:

- "Am I fully connected to my highest self and guides?"

- "Is my connection with the divine source of healing energy clear and strong?"

- "Is there anything else I need to do to ensure a strong connection for this session?"

If the pendulum swings positively to all questions, continue to the next step. If the pendulum swings negatively to any question, repeat the connection command and ask again until the pendulum confirms readiness.

IDENTIFY THE TRAUMATIC MEMORIES:

- "I now ask to be shown the specific traumatic memories that are ready to be healed. I invite these memories to surface in a way that is gentle, supportive, and safe for my healing."

PENDULUM QUESTIONS:

- "Has the traumatic memory been identified?"

- "Is this memory connected to a specific event?"

- "Is this memory connected to a series of events?"

- "Is this memory rooted in a past life experience?"

- "Are there multiple traumatic memories that need to be addressed?"

If the pendulum swings positively to the first question, proceed to the next step. If the pendulum swings negatively, allow more time for the information to surface and ask again.

CLEAR AND RELEASE THE TRAUMATIC MEMORY:

- "I now command that all trauma, pain, fear, and distress associated with this memory be fully cleared, released, and transmuted into pure love and light. I release all negative imprints, beliefs, and patterns formed as a result of this memory, sending them into the light for complete healing."

- "I command that any residual energy, emotions, or memories from this trauma be completely dissolved, never to return. I now fill the space left by this release with unconditional love, peace, and harmony."

- "I command that all physical imprints of this traumatic memory be erased from my cellular memory. My body is now free from any influence of this trauma."

- "I command that all emotional wounds caused by this memory be healed and transmuted into pure love. I release all emotional pain associated with this memory, allowing only love and peace to remain."

- "I command that all mental patterns formed as a result of this trauma be dissolved and replaced with thoughts of love, safety, and empowerment. My mind is now clear and aligned with my highest good."

- "I command that any energy cords or attachments related to this traumatic memory be fully severed and released. I am now free from any energetic ties to this memory or those involved."

PENDULUM QUESTIONS:

- "Has the traumatic memory been fully cleared and released?"

- "Are there any hidden or subconscious aspects of this memory that need to be addressed?"

- "Is there any energy from this trauma still lingering in my physical body?"

- "Is there any energy from this trauma still affecting my emotional body?"

- "Is there any energy from this trauma still influencing my mental body?"

If the pendulum swings positively to the first question and negatively to the others, move to the next step. If the pendulum swings positively to any of the follow-up questions, repeat the clearing commands specifically for the affected area until the pendulum confirms that the trauma has been released.

HEAL AND TRANSFORM

- "I now command that my entire being - body, mind, and spirit - be fully healed from the effects of this traumatic memory. I invite the energy of divine love and healing to fill every cell of my body, restoring perfect health, balance, and wholeness."

- "I command that any wounds, scars, or damage from this memory be completely healed, leaving no trace behind. I am reborn in perfect love and light."

- "I command that any energetic blockages caused by this memory be fully dissolved, allowing my energy to flow freely and harmoniously throughout my entire being."

- "I command that my energy field be fully restored, repaired, and strengthened. Any tears, holes, or weaknesses caused by this memory are now mended and fortified with divine love and light."

- "I command that my nervous system be fully balanced and calmed, releasing any tension or stress that may have resulted from this memory. I am now at peace, calm, and centered."

- "I command that my heart be fully opened to receiving and giving love, free from any fear or pain associated with this memory. My heart is now healed and overflowing with love and joy."

- "I command that my subconscious mind be reprogrammed with positive, empowering beliefs, free from any limiting beliefs formed by this traumatic memory."

- "I command that my inner child be fully healed, loved, and nurtured, free from any pain or fear caused by this trauma. My inner child is now safe, joyful, and at peace."

PENDULUM QUESTIONS:

- "Has the healing and transformation been fully completed?"

- "Is my physical body now fully healed from this memory?"

- "Is my emotional body now fully healed from this memory?"

- "Is my mental body now fully healed from this memory?"

- "Is my energy field fully restored and balanced?"

- "Is my subconscious mind now free from the influence of this memory?"

- "Are there any other aspects of my being that require healing?"

If the pendulum swings positively to the first question and negatively to the others, continue to the next step. If the pendulum swings positively to any of the follow-up questions, repeat the healing commands until the pendulum confirms completion.

SECURE THE FUTURE:

- "I now command that all future experiences be free from the influence of this traumatic memory. I secure my future with the energy of pure love, joy, and ease. My life is filled with positive, nurturing experiences that support my highest good."

- "I command that my future be aligned with my true purpose, mission, and highest potential, free from any past traumas. I am now fully empowered to live a life of peace, happiness, and fulfillment."

- "I command that any residual effects of this memory be fully neutralized and transmuted, ensuring they cannot influence my future in any way."

- "I command that all aspects of my life - relationships, health, career, and personal growth - be fully protected and aligned with my highest good, free from any lingering effects of this memory."

- "I command that my future self be empowered with strength, confidence, and resilience, ensuring that I am fully equipped to handle any challenges with grace and ease."

- "I command that any patterns or cycles that may have been formed by this memory be fully broken, ensuring they cannot repeat in my future."

PENDULUM QUESTIONS:

- "Is my future now secure and free from the influence of past traumatic memories?"

- "Are there any specific areas of my life that still need attention to secure my future?"

- "Is there anything else I need to do to fully secure my future?"

If the pendulum swings positively to the first question and negatively to the others, move to the closing. If the pendulum swings positively to any of the follow-up questions, repeat the securing commands as needed.

CLOSING THE SESSION:

- "I now disconnect from any energies, guides, or beings I connected with during this session. I am fully grounded, centered, and at peace. I thank all who assisted in this healing process. I am now free from the effects of any traumatic memories, and I step forward into my life with confidence, joy, and love."

- "I command that any residual energy from this session be fully integrated into my being in a harmonious and balanced way. I am now aligned with my highest good, and all aspects of my life reflect this alignment."

PENDULUM QUESTIONS:

- "Is the session now complete?"

- "Have all connections been fully and safely closed?"

- "Am I fully grounded and centered?"

2.

KARMIC WOUNDS WORKSHEETS

Karmic wounds are deep-seated emotional or spiritual injuries that stem from unresolved experiences in past lives. These wounds often manifest as recurring challenges, fears, or patterns in the present life, influencing how we respond to certain situations or relationships. Karmic wounds may carry the weight of past traumas, unfinished business, or lessons not yet learned, seeking resolution and healing. Addressing these wounds involves recognizing their origins, releasing the associated pain, and integrating the lessons they offer. Healing karmic wounds can lead to profound transformation, freeing the individual to live more fully in the present with greater clarity and purpose.

HEALING SESSION NO: 5

RECURRING PATTERNS

IDENTIFY THE RECURRING PATTERNS:

1. Is there a recurring pattern that needs to be addressed in my life? (Yes/No)

2. Is this pattern related to a specific area of my life? (Yes/No)

If Yes, ask: Is it related to (relationships, finances, health, career, spiritual growth, self-worth, etc.)? (Ask for each area individually)

3. Is this pattern connected to a specific belief or mindset I hold? (Yes/No)

4. Is there a specific event or trauma in my life that triggered this pattern? (Yes/No)

5. Did this pattern originate in a past life? (Yes/No)

6. Did this pattern originate in my current life?* (Yes/No)

7. Was this pattern inherited from my ancestors? (Yes/No)

8. Is this pattern influenced by external energies or entities? (Yes/No)

9. Is this pattern reinforced by any limiting beliefs or thought forms? (Yes/No)

10. Do I unconsciously perpetuate this pattern through my actions or decisions? (Yes/No)

REFLECTIVE QUESTIONS (JOURNAL):

- What recurring issues have I noticed in my life?

- How have these patterns affected my growth and happiness?

- What emotions or thoughts arise when I think about this pattern?

CLEARING THE ROOT CAUSE

- "I command to clear, release, and transmute the root cause of this recurring pattern from all levels of my being, including all associated beliefs, emotions, and energies."

- "I command to dissolve any attachments, cords, contracts, or vows that sustain this pattern, across all timelines, dimensions, and realities."

- "I command to neutralize any negative energy associated with this pattern, and replace it with pure love, light, and harmony."

- "I command to clear any external influences, entities, or energies that are contributing to the perpetuation of this pattern."

- "I command to release any resistance, fear, or doubt that is preventing the full healing and release of this pattern."

- "I command to dissolve any limiting beliefs or thought forms that are reinforcing this pattern in my life."

- "I command to send healing energy back in time to the moment this pattern was first established, clearing any emotional, mental, or energetic blockages that contributed to its formation."

- "I command to heal and release any unresolved trauma or emotions that are linked to this pattern, allowing for complete emotional and energetic freedom."

PENDULUM QUESTIONS:

1. Is there any resistance to releasing this pattern? (Yes/No)

2. Do I need to forgive someone or myself to fully release this pattern? (Yes/No)

If Yes, ask: I command to forgive and release all involved, sending love and light to all parties.

3. Is there any unresolved guilt, shame, or fear connected to this pattern? (Yes/No)

If Yes, command: "I command to clear, release, and transmute all guilt, shame, and fear related to this pattern.*

TRANSFORMING AND HARMONIZING:

- "I command to transform the energy of this pattern into positive, supportive energy that aligns with my highest good and true purpose."

- "I command to harmonize all aspects of my life that were affected by this pattern, bringing them into alignment with my true passion, purpose, mission, and overall well-being."

- "I command to strengthen my energy field, ensuring that this pattern cannot re-establish itself in the future."

- "I command to infuse my mind, body, and spirit with confidence, clarity, and positive energy, allowing me to make empowered choices moving forward."

- "I command to align my thoughts, emotions, and actions with the highest vibration of love, abundance, and success."

- "I command to activate and integrate new, positive patterns that support my growth, happiness, and fulfillment."

PENDULUM QUESTIONS:

1. Is there any additional healing needed to fully resolve this pattern? (Yes/No)

2. Is the energy surrounding this pattern now aligned with love, harmony, and positivity? (Yes/No)

3. Are there any other areas of my life that require harmonization following the release of this pattern? (Yes/No)

SECURING THE FUTURE

- "I command to secure my future, ensuring that no remnants of this pattern can affect me or re-manifest in any form."

- "I command to establish a protective shield around me, safeguarding me from any similar patterns, energies, or influences in the future."

- "I command to create a new pathway of growth, abundance, and positive experiences, free from the limitations of the past."

- "I command to anchor this new energy deeply into my subconscious mind, conscious mind, and energetic field, allowing me to fully embody this transformation."

- "I command to invite supportive energies, guides, and higher wisdom to assist me in maintaining this positive shift in my life."

FINAL QUESTIONS:

1. Is this healing session complete? (Yes/No)

2. Do I need to revisit this healing in the future?*
   (Yes/No)

3. Is there any additional guidance or action I need
   to take to ensure the complete release of this
   pattern? (Yes/No)

GRATITUDE AND REFLECTION

- I am deeply grateful for the healing and
  transformation that has taken place. I trust that my
  life is now free from this recurring pattern, and I
  am open to new, positive experiences.

CLOSING AFFIRMATION:

- I am free from all recurring patterns that no longer
  serve me. I am aligned with my highest good, and
  I welcome new, positive energies into my life.

HEALING SESSION NO: 6

PAST LIFE BLOCKAGES

IDENTIFYING PAST LIFE BLOCKAGES:

1. Are there any blockages from past lives that are currently affecting me? (Yes/No)

2. Is this blockage related to a specific area of my life? (Yes/No)

If Yes, ask: Is it related to (relationships, finances, health, career, spiritual growth, self-worth, etc.)? (Ask for each area individually)

3. Is this blockage connected to a specific past life event or trauma? (Yes/No)

4. Is this blockage linked to a vow, contract, or promise made in a past life? (Yes/No)

5. Is this blockage inherited from a past life lineage or ancestral line? (Yes/No)

6. Is this blockage associated with a specific belief or mindset carried over from a past life? (Yes/No)

7. Is there more than one past life contributing to this blockage? (Yes/No)

8. Is this blockage affecting my current relationships, opportunities, or personal growth? (Yes/No)

9. Does this blockage involve unresolved emotions such as fear, guilt, anger, or sadness from a past life? (Yes/No)

10. Is this blockage linked to a past life karmic debt or unresolved karma? (Yes/No)

REFLECTIVE QUESTIONS (JOURNAL):

- What patterns or issues have I noticed in my current life that may be linked to past life blockages?

- How do I feel when I consider the possibility of past life influences on my present situation?

CLEARING PAST LIFE BLOCKAGES:

- "I command to clear, release, and transmute the root cause of this blockage from all past lives, including all associated beliefs, emotions, and energies."

- "I command to dissolve any vows, contracts, promises, or agreements made in past lives that are no longer aligned with my highest good."

- "I command to clear any unresolved emotions or traumas from past lives that are contributing to this blockage, replacing them with healing and peace."

- "I command to neutralize any karmic debts or unresolved karma from past lives that are manifesting as blockages in my current life."

- "I command to release any limiting beliefs or thought forms that have carried over from past lives, and replace them with empowering, positive beliefs."

- "I command to clear any ancestral or lineage-based blockages from past lives, freeing my entire ancestral line from these limitations."

- "I command to send healing energy back to all past lives involved in this blockage, clearing and transforming any negative energies that were created."

- "I command to heal and release any attachments or cords that connect me to past life energies or entities that are no longer serving me."

PENDULUM QUESTIONS:

1. Is there any resistance to releasing this past life blockage? (Yes/No)

2. Do I need to forgive anyone or myself in order to fully release this blockage? (Yes/No)

If Yes, command: "I command to forgive and release all involved, sending love and light to all parties across all timelines and dimensions."

3. Is there any unresolved fear or guilt connected to this past life blockage? (Yes/No)

If Yes, command: "I command to clear, release, and transmute all fear and guilt associated with this past life blockage."

TRANSFORMING AND HARMONIZING:

- "I command to transform the energy of this past life blockage into positive, supportive energy that aligns with my highest good and true purpose."

- "I command to harmonize all aspects of my life that were affected by this past life blockage, bringing them into alignment with my true passion, purpose, and overall well-being."

- "I command to strengthen my energy field, ensuring that this past life blockage cannot re-establish itself in the future."

- "I command to integrate the lessons learned from this past life experience in a way that supports my growth and spiritual evolution in this lifetime."

- "I command to activate and integrate new, positive patterns that support my current life path and highest potential."

PENDULUM QUESTIONS:

1. Is there any additional healing needed to fully resolve this past life blockage? (Yes/No)

2. Is the energy surrounding this past life blockage now aligned with love, harmony, and positivity? (Yes/No)

3. Are there any other areas of my life that require harmonization following the release of this blockage? (Yes/No)

SECURING THE FUTURE

- "I command to secure my future, ensuring that no remnants of this past life blockage can affect me or re-manifest in any form."

- "I command to establish a protective shield around me, safeguarding me from any similar blockages, energies, or influences from past lives in the future."

- "I command to create a new pathway of growth, abundance, and positive experiences, free from the limitations of past life blockages."

- "I command to anchor this new energy deeply into my subconscious mind, conscious mind, and energetic field, allowing me to fully embody this transformation."

- "I command to invite supportive energies, guides, and higher wisdom to assist me in maintaining this positive shift in my life."

FINAL QUESTIONS:

- Is this healing session complete? (Yes/No)

- Do I need to revisit this healing in the future? (Yes/No)

- Is there any additional guidance or action I need to take to ensure the complete release of this past life blockage? (Yes/No)

GRATITUDE AND REFLECTION:

- "I am deeply grateful for the healing and transformation that has taken place. I trust that my life is now free from past life blockages, and I am open to new, positive experiences."

CLOSING AFFIRMATION:

- I am free from all past life blockages that no longer serve me. I am aligned with my highest good, and I welcome new, positive energies into my life.

HEALING SESSION NO: 7

SUBCONSCIOUS WOUNDS

IDENTIFYING SUBCONSCIOUS WOUNDS

1. Do I have subconscious wounds that need healing? (Yes/No)

2. Is this wound related to a specific area of my life? (Yes/No)

If Yes, ask: Is it related to (relationships, finances, health, self-worth, trauma, etc.)? (Ask for each area individually)

3. Did this wound originate in childhood? (Yes/No)

4. Is this wound connected to a specific event or trauma? (Yes/No)

5. Is this wound linked to a belief or mindset that I hold? (Yes/No)

6. Is this wound affecting my relationships or ability to trust others? (Yes/No)

7. Is this wound causing any self-sabotage or limiting behaviors? (Yes/No)

8. Is this wound inherited from my ancestors or family lineage? (Yes/No)

9. Is this wound related to a past life experience? (Yes/No)

10. Is this wound affecting my ability to manifest my desires?* (Yes/No)

REFLECTIVE QUESTIONS (JOURNAL):

- What recurring emotions or patterns have I noticed in my life that may be linked to subconscious wounds?

- How do these wounds manifest in my daily life and interactions?

HEALING SUBCONSCIOUS WOUNDS

- "I command to bring this subconscious wound into the light of awareness, so that it can be fully healed and released."

- "I command to clear, release, and transmute the root cause of this subconscious wound from all levels of my being, including all associated beliefs, emotions, and energies."

- "I command to heal any trauma or emotional pain associated with this wound, replacing it with love, peace, and understanding."

- "I command to dissolve any limiting beliefs or thought patterns that have formed as a result of this wound, and replace them with empowering, positive beliefs."

- "I command to release any stored emotions, such as fear, guilt, shame, or anger, that are connected to this wound, allowing them to be fully healed."

- "I command to clear any ancestral or lineage-based wounds that have been passed down to me, freeing my entire ancestral line from these limitations."

- "I command to heal and release any unresolved issues or emotions from past lives that are contributing to this wound."

- "I command to send healing energy to the original moment this wound was created, clearing and transforming any negative energies that were involved."

PENDULUM QUESTIONS:

1. Is there any resistance to healing this subconscious wound? (Yes/No)

2. Do I need to forgive anyone or myself to fully heal this wound? (Yes/No)

If Yes, command: "I command to forgive and release all involved, sending love and light to all parties across all timelines and dimensions."

3. Is there any unresolved fear or guilt connected to this wound? (Yes/No)

If Yes, command: "I command to clear, release, and transmute all fear and guilt associated with this wound."

TRANSFORMING AND HARMONIZING

- "I command to transform the energy of this wound into positive, supportive energy that aligns with my highest good and true purpose."

- "I command to harmonize all aspects of my life that were affected by this wound, bringing them into alignment with love, peace, and inner harmony."

- "I command to strengthen my energy field, ensuring that this wound cannot re-establish itself in the future."

- "I command to integrate the lessons learned from this wound in a way that supports my growth and emotional well-being."

- "I command to activate and integrate new, positive patterns that support my healing, empowerment, and self-love."

PENDULUM QUESTIONS:

1. Is there any additional healing needed to fully resolve this wound? (Yes/No)

2. Is the energy surrounding this wound now aligned with love, harmony, and positivity? (Yes/No)

3. Are there any other areas of my life that require harmonization following the healing of this wound? (Yes/No)

SECURING THE FUTURE:

- "I command to secure my future, ensuring that no remnants of this wound can affect me or re-manifest in any form."

- "I command to establish a protective shield around me, safeguarding me from any similar wounds, energies, or influences in the future."

- "I command to create a new pathway of growth, healing, and self-love, free from the limitations of subconscious wounds."

- "I command to anchor this new energy deeply into my subconscious mind, conscious mind, and energetic field, allowing me to fully embody this transformation."

- "I command to invite supportive energies, guides, and higher wisdom to assist me in maintaining this positive shift in my life."

FINAL QUESTIONS:

1. Is this healing session complete? (Yes/No)

2. Do I need to revisit this healing in the future? (Yes/No)

3. Is there any additional guidance or action I need to take to ensure the complete healing of this wound? (Yes/No)

GRATITUDE AND REFLECTION

- "I am deeply grateful for the healing and transformation that has taken place. I trust that my life is now free from subconscious wounds, and I am open to new, positive experiences."

REFLECTIVE QUESTIONS (JOURNAL):

1. How do I feel after this session?

2. What positive changes do I expect to see as a result of this healing?

3. What new patterns or behaviors do I want to cultivate in my life moving forward?

CLOSING AFFIRMATION:

- "I am free from all subconscious wounds that no longer serve me. I am aligned with my highest good, and I welcome new, positive energies into my life."

HEALING SESSION NO: 8

WOUNDED MASCULINE

IDENTIFYING WOUNDED MASCULINE ENERGY

1. Do I have wounded masculine energy that needs healing? (Yes/No)

2. Is this wounded energy affecting my relationships? (Yes/No)

3. Is this wounded energy influencing my career or finances? (Yes/No)

4. Is this wounded energy causing me to feel disconnected from my true self? (Yes/No)

5. Is this wounded energy manifesting as anger, control, or aggression? (Yes/No)

6. Is this wounded energy related to feelings of inadequacy or low self-worth? (Yes/No)

7. Is this wounded energy linked to a specific trauma or experience in my life?* (Yes/No)

8. Is this wounded energy inherited from my ancestors or family lineage? (Yes/No)

104

9. Is this wounded energy affecting my ability to take action or make decisions? (Yes/No)

10. Is this wounded energy blocking me from fully expressing my power and potential? (Yes/No)

REFLECTIVE QUESTIONS (JOURNAL):

- How do I perceive and express my masculine energy?

- What patterns or behaviors in my life might be linked to wounded masculine energy?

- How does this wounded energy affect my interactions with others and my sense of self?

HEALING WOUNDED MASCULINE ENERGY

- "I command to bring this wounded masculine energy into the light of awareness, so that it can be fully healed and balanced."

- "I command to clear, release, and transmute the root cause of this wounded masculine energy from all levels of my being, including all associated beliefs, emotions, and energies."

- "I command to heal any trauma, pain, or experiences that have contributed to the wounding of my masculine energy, replacing them with strength, confidence, and peace."

- "I command to dissolve any limiting beliefs or thought patterns that have formed as a result of wounded masculine energy, and replace them with empowering, positive beliefs."

- "I command to release any stored emotions, such as anger, resentment, fear, or inadequacy, that are connected to this wounded energy, allowing them to be fully healed."

- "I command to clear any ancestral or lineage-based wounds related to masculine energy, freeing my entire ancestral line from these limitations."

- "I command to heal and release any unresolved issues or emotions from past lives that are contributing to wounded masculine energy in this lifetime."

- "I command to send healing energy to the original moment this wounded energy was created, clearing and transforming any negative energies that were involved."

PENDULUM QUESTIONS:

1. Is there any resistance to healing this wounded masculine energy?* (Yes/No)

2. Do I need to forgive anyone or myself to fully heal this energy?* (Yes/No)

If Yes, command: "I command to forgive and release all involved, sending love and light to all parties across all timelines and dimensions."

3. Is there any unresolved fear, guilt, or shame connected to this wounded masculine energy?" (Yes/No)

If Yes, command: "I command to clear, release, and transmute all fear, guilt, and shame associated with this energy."

BALANCING AND HARMONIZING MASCULINE ENERGY

- "I command to transform this wounded masculine energy into healthy, balanced, and empowered masculine energy that supports my highest good."

- "I command to harmonize all aspects of my life that were affected by wounded masculine energy, bringing them into alignment with love, strength, and inner balance."

- "I command to strengthen my masculine energy, ensuring it is expressed in a healthy, positive way that honors my true self and highest potential."

- "I command to integrate the lessons learned from this healing process, allowing me to embody a balanced expression of both masculine and feminine energies."

- "I command to activate and integrate new, positive patterns that support my growth, empowerment, and self-confidence."

PENDULUM QUESTIONS:

1. Is there any additional healing needed to fully balance my masculine energy? (Yes/No)

2. Is the energy surrounding my masculine energy now aligned with love, harmony, and positivity? (Yes/No)

3. Are there any other areas of my life that require harmonization following the healing of this energy? (Yes/No)

SECURING THE FUTURE

- "I command to secure my future, ensuring that no remnants of wounded masculine energy can affect me or re-manifest in any form."

- "I command to establish a protective shield around me, safeguarding me from any similar wounds, energies, or influences in the future."

- "I command to create a new pathway of growth, strength, and self-confidence, free from the limitations of wounded masculine energy."

- "I command to anchor this new energy deeply into my subconscious mind, conscious mind, and energetic field, allowing me to fully embody this transformation."

- "I command to invite supportive energies, guides, and higher wisdom to assist me in maintaining a balanced expression of my masculine energy."

FINAL QUESTIONS:

1. Is this healing session complete? (Yes/No)

2. Do I need to revisit this healing in the future? (Yes/No)

3. Is there any additional guidance or action I need to take to ensure the complete healing of my masculine energy? (Yes/No)

GRATITUDE AND REFLECTION

- I am deeply grateful for the healing and transformation that has taken place. I trust that my masculine energy is now balanced and empowered, and I am open to new, positive experiences.

CLOSING AFFIRMATION:

- "I am free from all wounds related to my masculine energy. I embody a balanced, healthy expression of masculine energy, aligned with my highest good and true self.

HEALING SESSION NO: 9
WOUNDED FEMININE

IDENTIFYING WOUNDED FEMININE ENERGY

1. Do I have wounded feminine energy that needs healing? (Yes/No)

2. Is this wounded energy affecting my relationships? (Yes/No)

3. Is this wounded energy influencing my self-worth or self-esteem? (Yes/No)

4. Is this wounded energy causing me to feel disconnected from my emotions or intuition? (Yes/No)

5. Is this wounded energy manifesting as passivity, fear, or self-doubt? (Yes/No)

6. Is this wounded energy related to feelings of shame, guilt, or vulnerability? (Yes/No)

7. Is this wounded energy linked to a specific trauma or experience in my life? (Yes/No)

8. Is this wounded energy inherited from my ancestors or family lineage? (Yes/No)

9. Is this wounded energy affecting my ability to nurture myself or others? (Yes/No)

10. Is this wounded energy blocking me from fully expressing my creativity and potential? (Yes/No)

REFLECTIVE QUESTIONS (JOURNAL):

- How do I perceive and express my feminine energy?

- What patterns or behaviors in my life might be linked to wounded feminine energy?

- How does this wounded energy affect my sense of self, my relationships, and my creativity?

HEALING WOUNDED FEMININE ENERGY

- "I command to bring this wounded feminine energy into the light of awareness, so that it can be fully healed and balanced."

- "I command to clear, release, and transmute the root cause of this wounded feminine energy from all levels of my being, including all associated beliefs, emotions, and energies."

- "I command to heal any trauma, pain, or experiences that have contributed to the wounding of my feminine energy, replacing them with love, compassion, and peace."

- "I command to dissolve any limiting beliefs or thought patterns that have formed as a result of wounded feminine energy, and replace them with empowering, positive beliefs."

- "I command to release any stored emotions, such as shame, guilt, fear, or sadness, that are connected to this wounded energy, allowing them to be fully healed."

- "I command to clear any ancestral or lineage-based wounds related to feminine energy, freeing my entire ancestral line from these limitations."

- "I command to heal and release any unresolved issues or emotions from past lives that are contributing to wounded feminine energy in this lifetime."

- "I command to send healing energy to the original moment this wounded energy was created, clearing and transforming any negative energies that were involved."

PENDULUM QUESTIONS:

1. Is there any resistance to healing this wounded feminine energy? (Yes/No)

2. Do I need to forgive anyone or myself to fully heal this energy? (Yes/No)

If Yes, command: "I command to forgive and release all involved, sending love and light to all parties across all timelines and dimensions."

3. Is there any unresolved fear, guilt, or shame connected to this wounded feminine energy? (Yes/No)

If Yes, command: "I command to clear, release, and transmute all fear, guilt, and shame associated with this energy."

BALANCING AND HARMONIZING FEMININE ENERGY

- "I command to transform this wounded feminine energy into healthy, balanced, and empowered feminine energy that supports my highest good."

- "I command to harmonize all aspects of my life that were affected by wounded feminine energy, bringing them into alignment with love, intuition, and inner peace."

- "I command to strengthen my feminine energy, ensuring it is expressed in a healthy, positive way that honors my true self and highest potential."

- "I command to integrate the lessons learned from this healing process, allowing me to embody a balanced expression of both feminine and masculine energies."

- "I command to activate and integrate new, positive patterns that support my growth, empowerment, and self-love."

PENDULUM QUESTIONS:

1. Is there any additional healing needed to fully balance my feminine energy? (Yes/No)

2. Is the energy surrounding my feminine energy now aligned with love, harmony, and positivity? (Yes/No)

3. Are there any other areas of my life that require harmonization following the healing of this energy? (Yes/No)

SECURING THE FUTURE

- "I command to secure my future, ensuring that no remnants of wounded feminine energy can affect me or re-manifest in any form."

- "I command to establish a protective shield around me, safeguarding me from any similar wounds, energies, or influences in the future."

- "I command to create a new pathway of growth, love, and self-confidence, free from the limitations of wounded feminine energy."

- "I command to anchor this new energy deeply into my subconscious mind, conscious mind, and energetic field, allowing me to fully embody this transformation."

- "I command to invite supportive energies, guides, and higher wisdom to assist me in maintaining a balanced expression of my feminine energy."

FINAL QUESTIONS:

1. Is this healing session complete? (Yes/No)

2. Do I need to revisit this healing in the future? (Yes/No)

3. Is there any additional guidance or action I need to take to ensure the complete healing of my feminine energy? (Yes/No)

GRATITUDE AND REFLECTION

- "I am deeply grateful for the healing and transformation that has taken place. I trust that my feminine energy is now balanced and empowered, and I am open to new, positive experiences."

CLOSING AFFIRMATION:

- "I am free from all wounds related to my feminine energy. I embody a balanced, healthy expression of feminine energy, aligned with my highest good and true self."

HEALING SESSION NO: 10
WOUNDED INNER CHILD

CONNECTING WITH THE INNER CHILD

1. Is my inner child carrying wounds that need healing? (Yes/No)

2. Is there a specific age or period in my childhood where these wounds were formed? (Yes/No)

If Yes, ask: At what age did the most significant wounds occur? (You can ask age ranges if needed, e.g., 0-5 years, 6-10 years, etc.)

3. Are these wounds related to a specific event or experience in my childhood? (Yes/No)

4. Are these wounds affecting my current relationships or self-esteem? (Yes/No)

5. Are these wounds causing feelings of fear, abandonment, or unworthiness? (Yes/No)

6. Are these wounds linked to a belief that I am not loved, safe, or valued? (Yes/No)

7. Is my inner child feeling neglected or unheard? (Yes/No)

8. Are these wounds inherited from my parents or ancestors? (Yes/No)

116

9. Are these wounds affecting my ability to experience joy and playfulness? (Yes/No)

10. Are these wounds blocking me from fully expressing myself or pursuing my dreams? (Yes/No)

REFLECTIVE QUESTIONS (JOURNAL):

- What childhood memories or emotions come up when I think about my inner child?

- How do these memories influence my current behavior and feelings?

- What does my inner child need most from me right now?

HEALING THE WOUNDED INNER CHILD

- "I command to connect deeply with my inner child, bringing comfort, love, and understanding to this part of myself."

- "I command to clear, release, and transmute the root cause of these childhood wounds from all levels of my being, including all associated beliefs, emotions, and energies."

- "I command to heal any trauma, pain, or fear that my inner child experienced, replacing it with safety, love, and security."

- "I command to dissolve any limiting beliefs or thought patterns that were formed as a result of these childhood wounds, and replace them with empowering, positive beliefs."

- "I command to release any stored emotions, such as fear, sadness, or anger, that are connected to these wounds, allowing them to be fully healed."

- "I command to clear any ancestral or lineage-based wounds related to my inner child, freeing my entire ancestral line from these limitations."

- "I command to provide my inner child with the love, validation, and acceptance they needed but did not receive."

- "I command to send healing energy to the original moment these wounds were created, clearing and transforming any negative energies that were involved."

PENDULUM QUESTIONS:

1. Is there any resistance to healing these inner child wounds? (Yes/No)

2. Do I need to forgive anyone or myself to fully heal these wounds? (Yes/No)

If Yes, command: "I command to forgive and release all involved, sending love and light to all parties across all timelines and dimensions."

3. Is my inner child ready to receive healing and love? (Yes/No)

4. Does my inner child need anything specific to feel safe and loved? (Yes/No)

NURTURING AND REASSURING THE INNER CHILD

- "I command to nurture my inner child with unconditional love, care, and attention, allowing them to feel safe and cherished."

- "I command to reassure my inner child that they are now safe, loved, and valued, and that they can release any fears or insecurities they are holding."

- "I command to create a safe space within my heart where my inner child can play, express themselves, and feel joy."

- "I command to integrate the healed inner child energy into my adult self, bringing greater self-love, confidence, and emotional balance."

- "I command to activate and integrate new, positive patterns that support my inner child's growth, happiness, and well-being."

PENDULUM QUESTIONS:

1. Is there any additional healing needed to fully nurture and reassure my inner child? (Yes/No)

2. Is my inner child now feeling loved, safe, and valued? (Yes/No)

3. Are there any other areas of my life that require harmonization following the healing of my inner child? (Yes/No)

SECURING THE FUTURE

- "I command to secure my future, ensuring that no remnants of these inner child wounds can affect me or re-manifest in any form."

- "I command to establish a protective shield around my inner child, safeguarding them from any similar wounds, energies, or influences in the future."

- "I command to create a new pathway of growth, joy, and self-confidence, free from the limitations of childhood wounds."

- "I command to anchor this new energy deeply into my subconscious mind, conscious mind, and energetic field, allowing me to fully embody this transformation."

- "I command to invite supportive energies, guides, and higher wisdom to assist me in maintaining a healthy, loving relationship with my inner child."

FINAL QUESTIONS:

1. Is this healing session complete? (Yes/No)

2. Do I need to revisit this healing in the future? (Yes/No)

3. Is there any additional guidance or action I need to take to ensure the complete healing of my inner child? (Yes/No)

CLOSING:

- "I am deeply grateful for the healing and transformation that has taken place. I trust that my inner child is now loved, nurtured, and empowered, and I am open to new, positive experiences."

- "I am free from all wounds related to my inner child. I embody a balanced, loving relationship with my inner child, aligned with my highest good and true self.

PART 2:

RELATIONSHIP AND WEALTH HEALING

3.

RELATIONSHIP PATTERNS WORKSHEETS

Relationship patterns refer to the habitual ways in which individuals interact with others in their relationships, often reflecting deeper emotional or psychological themes. These patterns can be constructive, fostering closeness and understanding, or they can be destructive, leading to repeated conflicts, misunderstandings, or unfulfilled needs. Common patterns might include always taking on a caretaker role, struggling with trust, or repeatedly choosing similar types of partners. These patterns, often rooted in past experiences or unresolved issues, can unconsciously shape the course of relationships. By becoming aware of these recurring dynamics, individuals can work to change them, leading to healthier and more satisfying connections.

HEALING SESSION NO: 11
EMOTIONAL SAFETY

CURRENT EMOTIONAL STATE:

"Pendulum, am I currently experiencing any emotional blockages or disturbances that need to be addressed in this session?

- "Pendulum, please clear and release all negative emotional patterns, energies, and attachments that are blocking or hindering my sense of emotional safety. Transmute them into pure love and light."

"Pendulum, has all the negative emotional energy been fully cleared and released?"

ROOT CAUSES:

"Pendulum, are there any specific past events or traumas that are contributing to my feelings of emotional insecurity?"

- "Pendulum, please identify and release any past traumas, conscious or unconscious, that are impacting my emotional safety. Transmute these traumas into healing light, allowing me to feel safe and secure."

"Pendulum, has the trauma been fully released and healed?"

124

SUBCONSCIOUS INFLUENCES:

"Pendulum, are there any subconscious fears or limiting beliefs that are preventing me from feeling emotionally safe?"

- "Pendulum, identify and release any subconscious fears or beliefs that undermine my emotional safety. Replace these fears with a strong sense of peace and security."

"Pendulum, have all subconscious fears been cleared?"

HARMONIZATION AND BALANCE:

"Pendulum, are my emotional centers fully harmonized and balanced now?"

- "Pendulum, harmonize and balance my emotional body, aligning it with the highest frequency of love, peace, and security. Ensure all emotional centers are functioning optimally."

"Pendulum, has my emotional body been fully harmonized?"

STRENGTHENING BOUNDARIES:

"Pendulum, are my emotional boundaries strong and reinforced?"

- "Pendulum, please strengthen and reinforce my emotional boundaries. Create a protective energetic shield that allows only love, positivity, and support to enter, while repelling any negativity or harm."

"Pendulum, is my protective shield complete and effective?"

SUPPORTIVE RELATIONSHIPS:

"Pendulum, do the relationships in my life support my emotional safety?"

- "Pendulum, attract and amplify supportive, loving, and safe relationships in my life. Ensure all interactions are infused with mutual respect, understanding, and care."

"Pendulum, are these relationships now aligned with my emotional safety?"

ENHANCING SELF-LOVE AND CONFIDENCE:

"Pendulum, do I need to work on enhancing my self-love and self-confidence to feel more emotionally safe?"

- "Pendulum, enhance my self-love, self-worth, and confidence. Fill my being with unconditional love, ensuring I feel safe and secure within myself at all times."

"Pendulum, has my self-love and confidence been fully enhanced?"

CLEARING ANCESTRAL WOUNDS:

"Pendulum, are there any ancestral patterns or inherited emotional wounds affecting my sense of safety?"

- "Pendulum, clear and heal any ancestral emotional wounds or traumas that may be affecting my sense of emotional safety. Transmute these energies into healing light and restore balance across all timelines."

"Pendulum, has the ancestral healing been completed?"

EMPOWERING EMOTIONAL RESILIENCE:

"Pendulum, am I now better equipped to recover from emotional challenges?"

- "Pendulum, enhance my emotional resilience, enabling me to recover quickly and fully from any emotional challenges or disturbances."

"Pendulum, is my emotional resilience fully empowered?"

ANCHORING EMOTIONAL SAFETY:

"Pendulum, has the energy of emotional safety been successfully anchored into my future?"

- "Pendulum, anchor the energy of emotional safety deeply into my being, so that I always feel protected, loved, and secure, regardless of external circumstances."

"Pendulum, is this energy fully anchored in my present and future?"

DAILY PROTECTION:

"Pendulum, has daily energetic protection been established around me?"

- "Pendulum, establish a daily energetic protection around me that shields my emotional body from any negative influences or disturbances. Ensure that I remain emotionally safe and secure each day."

"Pendulum, is my daily protection strong and reliable?"

ACTIVATING EMOTIONAL INTUITION:

"Pendulum, is my emotional intuition fully activated and functioning?"

- "Pendulum, activate and enhance my emotional intuition, allowing me to recognize and respond to situations that support my emotional safety. Ensure I always make decisions that honor my emotional well-being."

"Pendulum, is my emotional intuition now fully activated?"

CLEARING ENERGETIC TIES:

"Pendulum, do I have any energetic ties or cords that are draining my emotional energy?"

- "Pendulum, please clear any negative or draining energetic ties or cords from past relationships or experiences that compromise my emotional safety. Transmute these ties into love and light, and restore my emotional energy to its fullest."

"Pendulum, have all energetic ties been cleared?"

INFUSING INNER PEACE:

"Pendulum, do I need to infuse more inner peace to enhance my emotional safety?"

- "Pendulum, infuse my entire being with the energy of inner peace and tranquility. Ensure that I remain calm, centered, and emotionally safe in all situations."

"Pendulum, is the energy of inner peace fully infused?"

HEALING EMOTIONAL BODY:

"Pendulum, is my emotional body in need of additional healing?"

- "Pendulum, heal any wounds, scars, or imbalances in my emotional body. Restore my emotional body to its perfect, healthy state, ensuring it vibrates with love, peace, and security."

"Pendulum, is my emotional body now fully healed?"

HARMONIZING MIND, BODY, AND SPIRIT:

"Pendulum, is there a need to further harmonize my mind, body, and spirit to support emotional safety?"

- "Pendulum, harmonize my mind, body, and spirit, ensuring they work together in perfect balance to maintain my emotional safety. Align all aspects of my being with the frequency of unconditional love and protection."

"Pendulum, are my mind, body, and spirit now in full harmony?"

AFFIRMATION:

- "I am safe, protected, and loved. My emotions are balanced, and I trust in my ability to navigate life with confidence and security."

HEALING SESSION NO: 12
HEARTBREAKS AND BETRAYAL

IDENTIFYING EMOTIONAL PAIN:

"Pendulum, am I currently holding onto emotional pain from heartbreak or betrayal?"

- "Pendulum, please identify and bring to the surface any emotional pain related to heartbreak or betrayal that I may be holding onto, whether consciously or unconsciously."

"Pendulum, has all emotional pain been fully identified?"

RELEASING PAINFUL EMOTIONS:

"Pendulum, am I ready to release the pain associated with heartbreak and betrayal?"

- "Pendulum, please clear and release all painful emotions, including sadness, anger, and grief, that have resulted from heartbreak or betrayal. Transmute these emotions into healing light and love."

"Pendulum, has all painful emotional energy been fully released?"

HEALING THE HEART:

"Pendulum, does my heart require healing from the wounds of betrayal?"

- "Pendulum, heal the wounds of my heart, sealing any cracks or scars caused by heartbreak and betrayal. Restore my heart to its full strength and capacity for love."

"Pendulum, has my heart been fully healed?"

RELEASING BETRAYAL ENERGY:

"Pendulum, am I holding onto any energy related to betrayal that is affecting my well-being?"

- "Pendulum, release and transmute all energy related to betrayal, including feelings of mistrust, resentment, and bitterness. Replace these energies with trust, forgiveness, and peace."

"Pendulum, has the energy of betrayal been fully transmuted?"

RESTORING TRUST:

"Pendulum, has my ability to trust been damaged by this experience?"

- "Pendulum, restore my ability to trust others and myself. Heal any wounds that have caused me to lose faith in relationships and in my own judgment."

"Pendulum, is my sense of trust fully restored?"

RELEASING ATTACHMENTS TO THE PAST:

"Pendulum, am I holding onto any attachments to the past that are keeping me from moving forward?"

- "Pendulum, release all attachments to the past, including any lingering thoughts, memories, or emotions tied to the person or situation that caused heartbreak or betrayal. Free me from the past so I can move forward."

"Pendulum, have all attachments to the past been fully released?"

HEALING BETRAYAL TRAUMA:

"Pendulum, do I have trauma from betrayal that needs to be healed?"

- "Pendulum, heal any trauma caused by betrayal, both conscious and subconscious. Transmute the energy of trauma into resilience and strength."

"Pendulum, has the trauma from betrayal been fully healed?"

FORGIVENESS:

"Pendulum, am I holding onto any unforgiveness towards myself or others related to this experience?"

- "Pendulum, assist me in fully forgiving myself and others involved in the betrayal or heartbreak. Release all energies of unforgiveness, and replace them with compassion, understanding, and inner peace."

"Pendulum, has forgiveness been fully achieved?"

REBUILDING SELF-LOVE:

"Pendulum, has this experience impacted my sense of self-love and self-worth?"

- "Pendulum, rebuild and enhance my self-love and self-worth, ensuring that I recognize my value and deserve healthy, loving relationships."

"Pendulum, is my sense of self-love and self-worth fully restored?"

CLEARING NEGATIVE BELIEFS:

"Pendulum, have I developed any negative beliefs about love, trust, or relationships because of this experience?"

- "Pendulum, clear any negative beliefs or patterns related to love, trust, and relationships that have formed as a result of this heartbreak or betrayal. Replace them with positive, empowering beliefs."

"Pendulum, have all negative beliefs been cleared and replaced?"

RECLAIMING PERSONAL POWER:

"Pendulum, have I lost any personal power due to this betrayal or heartbreak?"

- "Pendulum, help me reclaim my personal power that may have been lost or diminished due to heartbreak or betrayal. Empower me to move forward with confidence and strength."

"Pendulum, is my personal power fully reclaimed?"

CREATING HEALTHY BOUNDARIES:

"Pendulum, do I need to establish stronger boundaries to protect myself from future heartbreak?"

- "Pendulum, assist me in creating and maintaining healthy emotional boundaries to protect myself from future heartbreak or betrayal. Ensure these boundaries are strong yet flexible, allowing love and trust to flow freely."

"Pendulum, are my emotional boundaries now healthy and strong?"

RECONNECTING WITH JOY:

"Pendulum, have I lost touch with joy because of this experience?"

- "Pendulum, reconnect me with the energy of joy and happiness. Allow me to experience love and life with a renewed sense of optimism and enthusiasm."

"Pendulum, is the energy of joy fully restored in my life?"

PROJECTING HEALING INTO THE FUTURE:

"Pendulum, is my future free from the shadows of this heartbreak and betrayal?"

- "Pendulum, project healing, love, and trust into my future. Ensure that I enter future relationships with a healed heart and a positive outlook."

"Pendulum, is my future now aligned with healing and love?"

DAILY EMOTIONAL PROTECTION:

"Pendulum, do I need additional protection to guard against future emotional wounds?"

- "Pendulum, establish daily emotional protection to shield my heart from any future heartbreak or betrayal. Ensure that I remain emotionally safe and secure."

"Pendulum, is my daily emotional protection in place?"

HARMONIZING WITH DIVINE LOVE:

"Pendulum, am I fully aligned with the energy of divine love?"

- "Pendulum, harmonize my entire being with the energy of divine love, allowing me to attract and experience relationships that are based on unconditional love, respect, and mutual understanding."

"Pendulum, am I now fully aligned with divine love?"

AFFIRMATION:

"I am healed, whole, and free. I release the past and embrace my future with an open heart, filled with love, trust, and joy."

HEALING SESSION NO: 13

FEAR OF INTIMACY AND BETRAYAL

PURPOSE:

To heal and release fears related to intimacy and betrayal, fostering trust, openness, and emotional safety in relationships.

IDENTIFYING CORE FEARS:

"Pendulum, am I currently holding onto fears related to intimacy and betrayal?"

- "Pendulum, please identify and bring to the surface any fears related to intimacy and betrayal that I may be holding onto, whether consciously or unconsciously."

"Pendulum, have all core fears been fully identified?"

RELEASING FEAR OF INTIMACY:

"Pendulum, am I ready to release my fear of intimacy?"

- "Pendulum, please clear and release all fears related to intimacy, including fear of vulnerability, closeness, and emotional connection. Transmute these fears into love, trust, and openness."

"Pendulum, has the fear of intimacy been fully released?"

HEALING BETRAYAL WOUNDS:

"Pendulum, do I have unresolved wounds from past betrayals affecting my current relationships?"

- "Pendulum, heal any wounds caused by past betrayals, both conscious and subconscious. Transmute the energy of these wounds into strength, resilience, and wisdom."

"Pendulum, have all wounds from past betrayals been fully healed?"

RELEASING FEAR OF BETRAYAL:

"Pendulum, am I holding onto a fear of being betrayed in the future?"

- "Pendulum, release and transmute all fears of future betrayal. Replace these fears with trust, inner strength, and a sense of emotional safety."

"Pendulum, has the fear of betrayal been fully transmuted?"

RESTORING TRUST IN RELATIONSHIPS:

"Pendulum, has my ability to trust others been damaged by past experiences?"

- "Pendulum, restore my ability to trust others, allowing me to build healthy, supportive, and loving relationships. Heal any damage to my trust that has resulted from past betrayals."

"Pendulum, is my sense of trust in relationships fully restored?"

ENHANCING EMOTIONAL SAFETY:

"Pendulum, do I feel emotionally safe in my current relationships?"

- "Pendulum, enhance and reinforce my sense of emotional safety, ensuring that I feel secure, valued, and protected in all my relationships."

"Pendulum, is my sense of emotional safety fully enhanced?"

RELEASING ATTACHMENT TO PAST PAIN:

"Pendulum, am I holding onto any attachment to past pain or betrayal?"

- "Pendulum, release all attachments to past pain, betrayal, or hurtful experiences. Free me from the emotional burden of the past so I can embrace intimacy and trust in the present."

"Pendulum, have all attachments to past pain been fully released?"

HEALING EMOTIONAL SCARS:

"Pendulum, are there any emotional scars from past relationships that need healing?"

- "Pendulum, heal any emotional scars left by past relationships, restoring my emotional body to a state of wholeness and readiness for healthy intimacy."

"Pendulum, are my emotional scars fully healed?"

RECLAIMING PERSONAL POWER:

"Pendulum, have I lost any personal power due to fears of intimacy or past betrayals?"

- "Pendulum, help me reclaim my personal power that may have been diminished due to fears of intimacy or past betrayals. Empower me to engage in relationships with confidence and strength."

"Pendulum, is my personal power fully reclaimed?"

CLEARING NEGATIVE BELIEFS ABOUT INTIMACY:

"Pendulum, have I developed any negative beliefs about intimacy because of past experiences?"

- "Pendulum, clear any negative beliefs or patterns related to intimacy that have formed as a result of past betrayals or fears. Replace them with positive, empowering beliefs about connection and love."

"Pendulum, have all negative beliefs about intimacy been cleared and replaced?"

STRENGTHENING BOUNDARIES:

"Pendulum, do I need to strengthen my emotional boundaries to protect myself in future relationships?"

- "Pendulum, assist me in creating and maintaining healthy emotional boundaries that protect me from potential betrayal while allowing for deep intimacy and connection."

"Pendulum, are my emotional boundaries now healthy and strong?"

OPENING THE HEART TO LOVE:

"Pendulum, is my heart open to experiencing love and intimacy?"

- "Pendulum, gently open my heart to love and intimacy, ensuring that I am ready to give and receive love freely and fully, without fear of betrayal."

"Pendulum, is my heart fully open to love and intimacy?"

RELEASING CONTROL:

"Pendulum, am I trying to control relationships out of fear of being hurt?"

- "Pendulum, help me release any need to control relationships as a way to protect myself from potential hurt or betrayal. Allow me to trust the natural flow of love and connection."

"Pendulum, have I released the need to control relationships?"

FOSTERING VULNERABILITY:

"Pendulum, do I struggle with being vulnerable in relationships?"

- "Pendulum, foster a healthy sense of vulnerability in me, allowing me to share my true self with others without fear of judgment or betrayal."

"Pendulum, is my ability to be vulnerable in relationships now strong and balanced?"

PROJECTING HEALING INTO THE FUTURE:

"Pendulum, is my future free from the shadows of fear and betrayal?"

- "Pendulum, project healing, love, trust, and openness into my future. Ensure that I approach all future relationships with a healed heart and a positive outlook."

"Pendulum, is my future now aligned with healing and love?"

DAILY EMOTIONAL PROTECTION:

"Pendulum, do I need additional protection to guard against future emotional wounds?"

- "Pendulum, establish daily emotional protection to shield my heart from any future hurt or betrayal. Ensure that I remain emotionally safe and secure in all my interactions."

"Pendulum, is my daily emotional protection in place?"

HARMONIZING WITH DIVINE LOVE:

"Pendulum, am I fully aligned with the energy of divine love and intimacy?"

- "Pendulum, harmonize my entire being with the energy of divine love and intimacy, allowing me to attract and experience relationships that are based on unconditional love, respect, and mutual understanding."

"Pendulum, am I now fully aligned with divine love and intimacy?"

AFFIRMATION:

- "I am open to love and intimacy, trusting in the goodness of others and the strength within myself. I release the past and embrace my future with confidence and an open heart."

HEALING SESSION NO: 14

KARMIC RELATIONSHIPS

PURPOSE:

To heal and release the effects of karmic relationships, allowing for the integration of lessons, the dissolution of karmic ties, and the creation of healthy, balanced relationships in the present and future.

IDENTIFYING KARMIC TIES:

"Pendulum, am I currently involved in a karmic relationship?"

- "Pendulum, please identify and bring to the surface any karmic ties or relationships that are impacting my current life, whether consciously or unconsciously."

"Pendulum, have all karmic ties been fully identified?"

UNDERSTANDING THE LESSONS:

"Pendulum, is there a specific lesson I need to learn from this karmic relationship?"

- "Pendulum, help me understand and integrate the lessons from this karmic relationship, ensuring that I fully comprehend what is needed for my growth and evolution."

"Pendulum, have the lessons from this relationship been fully understood and integrated?"

RELEASING KARMIC DEBT:

"Pendulum, am I carrying any karmic debt from this relationship?"

- "Pendulum, release and transmute any karmic debt associated with this relationship. Free me from any lingering karmic obligations, allowing me to move forward with a clean slate."

"Pendulum, has all karmic debt been fully released and transmuted?"

HEALING EMOTIONAL WOUNDS:

"Pendulum, are there any emotional wounds from this karmic relationship that need healing?"

- "Pendulum, heal any emotional wounds that have resulted from this karmic relationship. Transmute the energy of these wounds into love, forgiveness, and inner peace."

"Pendulum, have all emotional wounds been fully healed?"

RELEASING NEGATIVE PATTERNS:

"Pendulum, have I developed any negative patterns or behaviors due to this karmic relationship?"

- "Pendulum, clear any negative patterns, behaviors, or beliefs that have formed as a result of this karmic relationship. Replace them with positive, empowering energies."

"Pendulum, have all negative patterns been cleared and replaced?"

DISSOLVING KARMIC TIES:

"Pendulum, is it time to dissolve the karmic ties from this relationship?"

- "Pendulum, dissolve all karmic ties associated with this relationship, freeing both parties to move forward in their own paths without further karmic entanglement."

"Pendulum, have all karmic ties been fully dissolved?"

FORGIVENESS AND COMPASSION:

"Pendulum, do I need to work on forgiveness and compassion in relation to this relationship?"

- "Pendulum, assist me in fully forgiving myself and the other person involved in this karmic relationship. Fill my heart with compassion, understanding, and love."

"Pendulum, is forgiveness and compassion fully achieved?"

RECLAIMING PERSONAL POWER

"Pendulum, have I lost any personal power due to this karmic relationship?"

- "Pendulum, help me reclaim my personal power that may have been lost or diminished due to this karmic relationship. Empower me to move forward with confidence and strength."

"Pendulum, is my personal power fully reclaimed?"

ANCESTRAL KARMIC PATTERNS:

"Pendulum, are there any ancestral karmic patterns influencing this relationship?"

- "Pendulum, clear any ancestral karmic patterns or influences that may be affecting this relationship. Transmute these patterns into pure love and light, freeing all involved."

"Pendulum, have all ancestral karmic patterns been cleared?"

STRENGTHENING BOUNDARIES:

"Pendulum, do I need to strengthen my boundaries in response to this karmic relationship?"

- "Pendulum, assist me in creating and maintaining strong, healthy boundaries that protect my energy and well-being, while allowing me to engage in balanced and respectful relationships."

"Pendulum, are my boundaries now healthy and strong?"

HEALING AND RELEASING PAST LIFE INFLUENCES:

"Pendulum, is this karmic relationship influenced by past life experiences?"

- "Pendulum, heal and release any past life influences that are contributing to this karmic relationship. Allow me to integrate the lessons from past lives and move forward without carrying any unresolved karma."

"Pendulum, have all past life influences been fully healed and released?"

BALANCING KARMA:

"Pendulum, is my karma balanced with this person?"

- "Pendulum, balance the karma between myself and the other person involved in this karmic relationship. Ensure that all karmic interactions are resolved in the highest and best way for all parties."

"Pendulum, is the karma between us now fully balanced?"

OPENING THE HEART:

"Pendulum, am I ready to open my heart to new, healthy relationships?"

- "Pendulum, gently open my heart to new relationships that are based on mutual love, respect, and understanding. Ensure that I am free from the influence of past karmic ties."

"Pendulum, is my heart fully open to new, healthy relationships?"

PROJECTING HEALING INTO THE FUTURE:

"Pendulum, is my future free from the influence of this karmic relationship?"

- "Pendulum, project healing, balance, and love into my future relationships. Ensure that I move forward free from the influence of past karma, ready to create positive, fulfilling connections."

"Pendulum, is my future now aligned with healing and balanced relationships?"

DAILY PROTECTION FROM KARMIC ENTANGLEMENTS:

"Pendulum, do I need protection from future karmic entanglements?"

- "Pendulum, establish daily protection around me to prevent any future karmic entanglements. Ensure that all my relationships are based on mutual respect, love, and positive energy."

"Pendulum, is my daily protection in place?"

HARMONIZING WITH DIVINE LOVE AND WISDOM:

"Pendulum, am I fully aligned with the energy of divine love and wisdom in my relationships?"

- "Pendulum, harmonize my entire being with the energy of divine love and wisdom, allowing me to attract and maintain relationships that support my highest good and spiritual growth."

"Pendulum, am I now fully aligned with divine love and wisdom in my relationships?"

AFFIRMATION:

- "I am free from past karmic ties and fully aligned with love, wisdom, and balance. I welcome healthy, fulfilling relationships into my life, grounded in mutual respect and understanding."

HEALING SESSION NO: 15

SEPARATION AND BREAKUPS

PURPOSE:

To heal the emotional and energetic wounds from separation and breakup, allowing you to release the past, regain balance, and embrace a future filled with self-love, peace, and new opportunities.

IDENTIFYING EMOTIONAL PAIN:

"Pendulum, am I currently holding onto emotional pain from this separation or breakup?"

- "Pendulum, please identify and bring to the surface any emotional pain related to this separation or breakup, whether consciously or unconsciously."

"Pendulum, has all emotional pain been fully identified?"

RELEASING EMOTIONAL PAIN:

"Pendulum, am I ready to release the emotional pain associated with this separation or breakup?"

- "Pendulum, please clear and release all emotional pain, including sadness, grief, and anger, that has resulted from this separation or breakup. Transmute these emotions into healing light and inner peace."

"Pendulum, has all emotional pain been fully released?"

HEALING THE HEART:

"Pendulum, does my heart require healing from the wounds of this breakup?"

- "Pendulum, heal the wounds of my heart, sealing any cracks or scars caused by this separation or breakup. Restore my heart to its full strength and capacity for love."

"Pendulum, has my heart been fully healed?"

RELEASING ATTACHMENTS TO THE PAST:

"Pendulum, am I holding onto any attachments to the past that are keeping me from moving forward?"

- "Pendulum, release all attachments to the past, including any lingering thoughts, memories, or emotions tied to the person or situation that caused the breakup. Free me from the past so I can move forward."

"Pendulum, have all attachments to the past been fully released?"

HEALING AND RELEASING ENERGETIC TIES:

"Pendulum, do I have any lingering energetic ties to this person that are affecting my well-being?"

- "Pendulum, clear and release any energetic ties or cords between myself and the person involved in this separation. Transmute these ties into love and light, restoring my energy to its fullness."

"Pendulum, have all energetic ties been fully released?"

REBUILDING SELF-WORTH AND CONFIDENCE:

"Pendulum, has this breakup affected my self-worth and confidence?"

- "Pendulum, rebuild and enhance my self-worth and confidence, ensuring that I recognize my value and deserve healthy, loving relationships."

"Pendulum, is my self-worth and confidence fully restored?"

RELEASING GUILT AND REGRET:

"Pendulum, am I holding onto any guilt or regret related to this separation or breakup?"

- "Pendulum, release all feelings of guilt, regret, or self-blame associated with this separation or breakup. Replace these emotions with forgiveness, understanding, and self-compassion."

"Pendulum, have guilt and regret been fully released?"

FORGIVING AND LETTING GO:

"Pendulum, do I need to forgive myself or the other person involved in this breakup?"

- "Pendulum, assist me in fully forgiving myself and the other person involved in this separation. Release all energies of unforgiveness, and replace them with peace, understanding, and closure."

"Pendulum, is forgiveness and letting go fully achieved?"

RESTORING EMOTIONAL BALANCE:

"Pendulum, is my emotional body in need of balance after this breakup?"

- "Pendulum, restore balance and harmony to my emotional body, ensuring that I am emotionally grounded and centered following this breakup."

"Pendulum, is my emotional balance fully restored?"

RECLAIMING PERSONAL POWER:

"Pendulum, have I lost any personal power due to this separation or breakup?"

- "Pendulum, help me reclaim my personal power that may have been lost or diminished due to this breakup. Empower me to move forward with confidence and strength."

"Pendulum, is my personal power fully reclaimed?"

CLEARING NEGATIVE BELIEFS ABOUT RELATIONSHIPS:

"Pendulum, have I developed any negative beliefs about relationships because of this breakup?"

- "Pendulum, clear any negative beliefs or patterns related to relationships that have formed as a result of this separation. Replace them with positive, empowering beliefs about love and connection."

"Pendulum, have all negative beliefs about relationships been cleared and replaced?"

OPENING THE HEART TO NEW LOVE:

"Pendulum, am I ready to open my heart to new love and relationships?"

- "Pendulum, gently open my heart to new love and relationships, ensuring that I am ready to give and receive love freely and fully, without fear or hesitation."

"Pendulum, is my heart fully open to new love and relationships?"

CREATING HEALTHY BOUNDARIES:

"Pendulum, do I need to establish stronger boundaries to protect myself in future relationships?"

- "Pendulum, assist me in creating and maintaining healthy emotional boundaries that protect me in future relationships while allowing love and trust to flow freely."

"Pendulum, are my emotional boundaries now healthy and strong?"

RECONNECTING WITH JOY:

"Pendulum, have I lost touch with joy because of this breakup?"

- "Pendulum, reconnect me with the energy of joy and happiness. Allow me to experience life with a renewed sense of optimism and enthusiasm."

"Pendulum, is the energy of joy fully restored in my life?"

PROJECTING HEALING INTO THE FUTURE:

"Pendulum, is my future free from the shadows of this breakup?"

- "Pendulum, project healing, love, and new opportunities into my future. Ensure that I move forward free from the influence of this breakup, ready to embrace new possibilities."

"Pendulum, is my future now aligned with healing and love?"

DAILY EMOTIONAL PROTECTION:

"Pendulum, do I need additional protection to guard against future emotional wounds?"

- "Pendulum, establish daily emotional protection to shield my heart from any future hurt or betrayal. Ensure that I remain emotionally safe and secure."

"Pendulum, is my daily emotional protection in place?"

HARMONIZING WITH DIVINE LOVE:

"Pendulum, am I fully aligned with the energy of divine love and wisdom?"

- "Pendulum, harmonize my entire being with the energy of divine love and wisdom, allowing me to attract and experience relationships that support my highest good and spiritual growth."

"Pendulum, am I now fully aligned with divine love and wisdom?"

AFFIRMATION:

"I release the past with love and embrace my future with an open heart. I am whole, healed, and ready for new love and joy in my life."

HEALING SESSION NO: 16

BREAKUPS AND DIVORCE

PURPOSE:

To heal the emotional and energetic wounds from breakups and divorce, allowing you to release the past, regain balance, and embrace a future filled with self-love, peace, and new opportunities.

IDENTIFYING EMOTIONAL PAIN:

"Pendulum, am I currently holding onto emotional pain from this breakup or divorce?"

- "Pendulum, please identify and bring to the surface any emotional pain related to this breakup or divorce, whether consciously or unconsciously."

"Pendulum, has all emotional pain been fully identified?"

RELEASING EMOTIONAL PAIN:

"Pendulum, am I ready to release the emotional pain associated with this breakup or divorce?"

- "Pendulum, please clear and release all emotional pain, including sadness, grief, and anger, that has resulted from this breakup or divorce. Transmute these emotions into healing light and inner peace."

"Pendulum, has all emotional pain been fully released?"

HEALING THE HEART:

"Pendulum, does my heart require healing from the wounds of this breakup or divorce?"

- "Pendulum, heal the wounds of my heart, sealing any cracks or scars caused by this breakup or divorce. Restore my heart to its full strength and capacity for love."

"Pendulum, has my heart been fully healed?"

RELEASING ATTACHMENTS TO THE PAST:

"Pendulum, am I holding onto any attachments to the past that are keeping me from moving forward?"

- "Pendulum, release all attachments to the past, including any lingering thoughts, memories, or emotions tied to the person or situation that caused the breakup or divorce. Free me from the past so I can move forward."

"Pendulum, have all attachments to the past been fully released?"

HEALING AND RELEASING ENERGETIC TIES:

"Pendulum, do I have any lingering energetic ties to this person that are affecting my well-being?"

- "Pendulum, clear and release any energetic ties or cords between myself and the person involved in this breakup or divorce. Transmute these ties into love and light, restoring my energy to its fullness."

"Pendulum, have all energetic ties been fully released?"

REBUILDING SELF-WORTH AND CONFIDENCE:

"Pendulum, has this breakup or divorce affected my self-worth and confidence?"

- "Pendulum, rebuild and enhance my self-worth and confidence, ensuring that I recognize my value and deserve healthy, loving relationships."

"Pendulum, is my self-worth and confidence fully restored?"

RELEASING GUILT AND REGRET:

"Pendulum, am I holding onto any guilt or regret related to this breakup or divorce?"

- "Pendulum, release all feelings of guilt, regret, or self-blame associated with this breakup or divorce. Replace these emotions with forgiveness, understanding, and self-compassion."

"Pendulum, have guilt and regret been fully released?"

FORGIVING AND LETTING GO:

"Pendulum, do I need to forgive myself or the other person involved in this breakup or divorce?"

- "Pendulum, assist me in fully forgiving myself and the other person involved in this breakup or divorce. Release all energies of unforgiveness, and replace them with peace, understanding, and closure."

"Pendulum, is forgiveness and letting go fully achieved?"

RESTORING EMOTIONAL BALANCE:

"Pendulum, is my emotional body in need of balance after this breakup or divorce?"

- "Pendulum, restore balance and harmony to my emotional body, ensuring that I am emotionally grounded and centered following this breakup or divorce."

"Pendulum, is my emotional balance fully restored?"

RECLAIMING PERSONAL POWER:

"Pendulum, have I lost any personal power due to this breakup or divorce?"

- "Pendulum, help me reclaim my personal power that may have been lost or diminished due to this breakup or divorce. Empower me to move forward with confidence and strength."

"Pendulum, is my personal power fully reclaimed?"

CLEARING NEGATIVE BELIEFS ABOUT RELATIONSHIPS:

"Pendulum, have I developed any negative beliefs about relationships because of this breakup or divorce?"

- "Pendulum, clear any negative beliefs or patterns related to relationships that have formed as a result of this breakup or divorce. Replace them with positive, empowering beliefs about love and connection."

"Pendulum, have all negative beliefs about relationships been cleared and replaced?"

HEALING FAMILY DYNAMICS:

"Pendulum, have any family dynamics been negatively impacted by this breakup or divorce?"

- "Pendulum, heal and restore harmony to any family dynamics affected by this breakup or divorce. Ensure that all family members find peace and understanding."

"Pendulum, are family dynamics fully healed and harmonized?"

OPENING THE HEART TO NEW LOVE:

"Pendulum, am I ready to open my heart to new love and relationships?"

- "Pendulum, gently open my heart to new love and relationships, ensuring that I am ready to give and receive love freely and fully, without fear or hesitation."

"Pendulum, is my heart fully open to new love and relationships?"

CREATING HEALTHY BOUNDARIES:

"Pendulum, do I need to establish stronger boundaries to protect myself in future relationships?"

- "Pendulum, assist me in creating and maintaining healthy emotional boundaries that protect me in future relationships while allowing love and trust to flow freely."

"Pendulum, are my emotional boundaries now healthy and strong?"

RECONNECTING WITH JOY:

"Pendulum, have I lost touch with joy because of this breakup or divorce?"

- "Pendulum, reconnect me with the energy of joy and happiness. Allow me to experience life with a renewed sense of optimism and enthusiasm."

"Pendulum, is the energy of joy fully restored in my life?"

PROJECTING HEALING INTO THE FUTURE:

"Pendulum, is my future free from the shadows of this breakup or divorce?"

- "Pendulum, project healing, love, and new opportunities into my future. Ensure that I move forward free from the influence of this breakup or divorce, ready to embrace new possibilities."

"Pendulum, is my future now aligned with healing and love?"

DAILY EMOTIONAL PROTECTION:

"Pendulum, do I need additional protection to guard against future emotional wounds?"

- "Pendulum, establish daily emotional protection to shield my heart from any future hurt or betrayal. Ensure that I remain emotionally safe and secure."

"Pendulum, is my daily emotional protection in place?"

HARMONIZING WITH DIVINE LOVE:

"Pendulum, am I fully aligned with the energy of divine love and wisdom?"

- "Pendulum, harmonize my entire being with the energy of divine love and wisdom, allowing me to attract and experience relationships that support my highest good and spiritual growth."

"Pendulum, am I now fully aligned with divine love and wisdom?"

- "I release the past with love and embrace my future with an open heart. I am whole, healed, and ready for new love and joy in my life."

4.

PROSPERITY

WORKSHEETS

Prosperity is the experience of thriving and abundance in all areas of life, from financial wealth to personal fulfillment. It embodies a sense of growth, where opportunities, success, and happiness are continually expanding. Prosperity is not just about accumulating material wealth; it's about living a balanced and enriched life where one's needs and desires are met with ease. It often reflects a state of harmony, where resources, relationships, and health are in alignment, creating a foundation for sustained well-being and joy. True prosperity is about cultivating a mindset of abundance, where gratitude and generosity play key roles in attracting and maintaining this state of flourishing.

HEALING SESSION NO: 17

SCARCITY MINDSET

OBJECTIVE:

To release the limiting beliefs and energetic blocks associated with scarcity, transforming them into an abundant mindset that attracts prosperity, wealth, and opportunities.

CLEARING THE SCARCITY MINDSET:

- "I command to clear, release, and transmute all energetic blocks, limiting beliefs, and subconscious patterns related to scarcity in all aspects of my being across all dimensions, lifetimes, and timelines, into pure love and light."

- "I command to dissolve all ancestral, genetic, and karmic ties to scarcity and lack, freeing my lineage and soul from these limiting patterns."

- "I command to clear all energetic imprints of poverty consciousness from my energy field and cellular memory, transmuting them into pure abundance and prosperity."

"Are there any specific memories, past lives, or inherited patterns contributing to my scarcity mindset?"

"Is there a particular aspect of my life where the scarcity mindset is most deeply rooted?"

- "I release all fears and beliefs rooted in scarcity. I am free from the limitations of lack."

"Is there any remaining energetic block or belief related to scarcity that needs to be cleared?"

- "I command to clear any remaining energetic block or belief related to scarcity and transmute it into pure love and light."

ACTIVATING ABUNDANCE CONSCIOUSNESS:

- "I command to activate, amplify, and integrate a mindset of abundance, prosperity, and unlimited possibilities within my conscious and subconscious mind."

- "I command to reprogram my mind to automatically perceive opportunities, wealth, and abundance in all situations and interactions."

- "I command to instill a deep sense of deservingness and self-worth, aligning me with the frequency of prosperity and abundance."

"Is my conscious mind fully aligned with the abundance mindset?"

"Is my subconscious mind accepting and integrating the abundance mindset without resistance?"

- "I embrace an abundant mindset. Opportunities, wealth, and prosperity flow effortlessly to me."

"Has the abundance mindset been fully activated and integrated?"

- "I command to further enhance the activation of an abundance mindset until it is fully integrated."

HARMONIZING ABUNDANCE WITH ALL ASPECTS OF LIFE:

- "I command to harmonize and align my abundant mindset with all aspects of my life - financial, emotional, mental, spiritual, and physical - for the highest good."

- "I command to align my thoughts, emotions, and actions with the flow of abundance, ensuring I am always in harmony with the prosperity that surrounds me."

- "I command to clear any energetic blocks or resistances within my relationships, career, and personal growth that may hinder the full expression of my abundance mindset."

"Is there any area of my life that is resisting the abundance mindset?"

"Are there specific relationships or situations that need additional harmonization with my abundance mindset?"

- "My abundant mindset positively influences every area of my life. I am in harmony with the flow of prosperity."

"Is there any resistance or disharmony in any aspect of my life regarding the abundance mindset?"

- "I command to clear all resistance and harmonize the abundance mindset with every aspect of my life."

ENSURING LONGEVITY AND EFFECTIVENESS:

- "I command to ensure the longevity and continuous effectiveness of this abundance mindset, allowing it to grow and strengthen over time."

- "I command to reinforce and solidify my connection to the universal flow of abundance, ensuring it becomes a permanent aspect of my being."

- "I command to continuously attract and manifest experiences that reinforce my abundance mindset and bring prosperity into my life."

"Will my abundance mindset continue to grow and strengthen over time?"

"Are there any future challenges or situations where my abundance mindset needs additional support?"

- "My abundance mindset continues to grow and strengthen every day. I am open to receiving and giving in equal measure."

"Is there anything else needed to ensure the continuous effectiveness of this abundance mindset?"

- "I command to make any necessary adjustments to ensure the continuous effectiveness of this abundance mindset."

CLOSING THE SESSION:

- Take a moment to express gratitude for the healing and transformation that has taken place.

- Ground yourself by taking a few deep breaths and slowly bringing your awareness back to the present moment.

- Journal any thoughts, feelings, or insights that arose during the session.

- Reflect on how you can incorporate the abundance mindset into your daily life.

HEALING SESSION NO: 18
POVERTY MINDSET

OBJECTIVE:

To release the limiting beliefs and energetic blocks associated with poverty, transforming them into a mindset that attracts wealth, security, and financial freedom.

CLEARING THE POVERTY MINDSET:

- "I command to clear, release, and transmute all energetic blocks, limiting beliefs, and subconscious patterns related to poverty in all aspects of my being across all dimensions, lifetimes, and timelines, into pure love and light."

- "I command to dissolve all ancestral, genetic, and karmic ties to poverty and financial struggle, freeing my lineage and soul from these limiting patterns."

- "I command to clear all energetic imprints of poverty consciousness from my energy field, cellular memory, and genetic code, transmuting them into wealth, security, and financial freedom."

"Are there any specific memories, past lives, or inherited patterns contributing to my poverty mindset?"

"Is there a particular aspect of my life where the poverty mindset is most deeply rooted?"

- "I release all fears and beliefs rooted in poverty. I am free from the limitations of financial struggle."

"Is there any remaining energetic block or belief related to poverty that needs to be cleared?"

- "I command to clear any remaining energetic block or belief related to poverty and transmute it into pure love and light."

ACTIVATING WEALTH CONSCIOUSNESS:

- "I command to activate, amplify, and integrate a mindset of wealth, financial security, and unlimited financial possibilities within my conscious and subconscious mind."

- "I command to reprogram my mind to automatically perceive wealth, security, and financial opportunities in all situations and interactions."

- "I command to instill a deep sense of deservingness and self-worth, aligning me with the frequency of financial abundance and security."

"Is my conscious mind fully aligned with the wealth mindset?"

"Is my subconscious mind accepting and integrating the wealth mindset without resistance?"

- "I embrace a wealth mindset. Financial opportunities, security, and abundance flow effortlessly to me."

"Has the wealth mindset been fully activated and integrated?"

- "I command to further enhance the activation of a wealth mindset until it is fully integrated."

HARMONIZING WEALTH WITH ALL ASPECTS OF LIFE:

- "I command to harmonize and align my wealth mindset with all aspects of my life - financial, emotional, mental, spiritual, and physical - for the highest good."

- "I command to align my thoughts, emotions, and actions with the flow of wealth, ensuring I am always in harmony with financial security and abundance."

- "I command to clear any energetic blocks or resistances within my relationships, career, and personal growth that may hinder the full expression of my wealth mindset."

"Is there any area of my life that is resisting the wealth mindset?"

"Are there specific relationships or situations that need additional harmonization with my wealth mindset?"

- "My wealth mindset positively influences every area of my life. I am in harmony with the flow of financial abundance and security."

"Is there any resistance or disharmony in any aspect of my life regarding the wealth mindset?"

- "I command to clear all resistance and harmonize the wealth mindset with every aspect of my life."

ENSURING LONGEVITY AND EFFECTIVENESS:

- "I command to ensure the longevity and continuous effectiveness of this wealth mindset, allowing it to grow and strengthen over time."

- "I command to reinforce and solidify my connection to the universal flow of wealth and financial security, ensuring it becomes a permanent aspect of my being."

- "I command to continuously attract and manifest experiences that reinforce my wealth mindset and bring financial security and abundance into my life."

"Will my wealth mindset continue to grow and strengthen over time?"

"Are there any future challenges or situations where my wealth mindset needs additional support?"

- "My wealth mindset continues to grow and strengthen every day. I am open to receiving and giving in equal measure."

"Is there anything else needed to ensure the continuous effectiveness of this wealth mindset?"

- "I command to make any necessary adjustments to ensure the continuous effectiveness of this wealth mindset."

CLOSING THE SESSION:

- Take a moment to express gratitude for the healing and transformation that has taken place.

- Ground yourself by taking a few deep breaths and slowly bringing your awareness back to the present moment.

- Journal any thoughts, feelings, or insights that arose during the session.

- Reflect on how you can incorporate the wealth mindset into your daily life.

HEALING SESSION NO: 19

VICTIM MENTALITY

OBJECTIVE:

To release the limiting beliefs and energetic blocks associated with victim mentality, empowering you to reclaim your personal power and embrace a mindset of strength, resilience, and self-empowerment.

CLEARING THE VICTIM MENTALITY:

- "I command to clear, release, and transmute all energetic blocks, limiting beliefs, and subconscious patterns related to victim mentality in all aspects of my being across all dimensions, lifetimes, and timelines, into pure love and light."

- "I command to dissolve all ancestral, genetic, and karmic ties to victimhood, freeing my lineage and soul from these limiting patterns."

- "I command to clear all energetic imprints of powerlessness, helplessness, and self-pity from my energy field, cellular memory, and genetic code, transmuting them into strength, resilience, and self-empowerment."

"Are there any specific memories, past lives, or inherited patterns contributing to my victim mentality?"

"Is there a particular area of my life where the victim mentality is most deeply rooted?"

174

- "I release all beliefs and patterns rooted in victimhood. I reclaim my power and embrace my strength."

"Is there any remaining energetic block or belief related to victim mentality that needs to be cleared?"

- "I command to clear any remaining energetic block or belief related to victim mentality and transmute it into pure love and light."

ACTIVATING EMPOWERMENT CONSCIOUSNESS:

- "I command to activate, amplify, and integrate a mindset of empowerment, resilience, and self-determination within my conscious and subconscious mind."

- "I command to reprogram my mind to automatically perceive challenges as opportunities for growth and empowerment."

- "I command to instill a deep sense of personal responsibility and the power to create my reality, aligning me with the frequency of self-empowerment and resilience."

"Is my conscious mind fully aligned with the empowerment mindset?"

"Is my subconscious mind accepting and integrating the empowerment mindset without resistance?"

- "I embrace an empowerment mindset. I have the power to overcome challenges and create my desired reality."

"Has the empowerment mindset been fully activated and integrated?"

- "I command to further enhance the activation of an empowerment mindset until it is fully integrated."

HARMONIZING EMPOWERMENT WITH ALL ASPECTS OF LIFE:

- "I command to harmonize and align my empowerment mindset with all aspects of my life - emotional, mental, spiritual, and physical - for the highest good."

- "I command to align my thoughts, emotions, and actions with the flow of empowerment, ensuring I am always in harmony with my inner strength and resilience."

- "I command to clear any energetic blocks or resistances within my relationships, career, and personal growth that may hinder the full expression of my empowerment mindset."

"Is there any area of my life that is resisting the empowerment mindset?"

"Are there specific relationships or situations that need additional harmonization with my empowerment mindset?"

- "My empowerment mindset positively influences every area of my life. I am in harmony with my strength and resilience."

"Is there any resistance or disharmony in any aspect of my life regarding the empowerment mindset?"

- "I command to clear all resistance and harmonize the empowerment mindset with every aspect of my life."

ENSURING LONGEVITY AND EFFECTIVENESS:

- "I command to ensure the longevity and continuous effectiveness of this empowerment mindset, allowing it to grow and strengthen over time."

- "I command to reinforce and solidify my connection to my inner power and resilience, ensuring they become a permanent aspect of my being."

- "I command to continuously attract and manifest experiences that reinforce my empowerment mindset and strengthen my personal power."

"Will my empowerment mindset continue to grow and strengthen over time?"

"Are there any future challenges or situations where my empowerment mindset needs additional support?"

- "My empowerment mindset continues to grow and strengthen every day. I am open to embracing my power and using it wisely."

"Is there anything else needed to ensure the continuous effectiveness of this empowerment mindset?"

- "I command to make any necessary adjustments to ensure the continuous effectiveness of this empowerment mindset."

CLOSING THE SESSION:

- Take a moment to express gratitude for the healing and transformation that has taken place.

- Ground yourself by taking a few deep breaths and slowly bringing your awareness back to the present moment.

PART 3:

MIND, BODY, EMOTIONS HEALING

5.

PHYSICAL HEALING WORKSHEETS

Physical healing, whether from illness or in improving appearance, involves the body's remarkable ability to repair, regenerate, and restore itself. Recovering from illness requires the body to combat infections, rebuild tissues, and regain strength, often aided by treatments, proper nutrition, and rest. In terms of appearance, physical healing can mean revitalizing the skin, reducing scars, or enhancing overall vitality, reflecting the body's inner health. Both aspects of healing are deeply connected, as true physical recovery encompasses not just the absence of illness, but also the restoration of a healthy, radiant appearance.

HEALING CONCEPT NO: 20

SKIN ISSUES

SET YOUR INTENTION:

- "I intend to address and heal any skin issues from the past, present, and future, transforming them into pure love and light, bringing forth radiant, healthy, and beautiful skin."

INVOKE DIVINE ASSISTANCE:

- "I call upon the highest divine energies, my guides, angels, and higher self, to assist in this healing session. May this session be for the highest good, in accordance with divine will."

ADDRESSING PAST LIFE SKIN ISSUES

- "Pendulum, please connect to all past life memories, experiences, and energies related to skin issues."

- "Clear and release all past life traumas, scars, and negative imprints associated with skin issues. Transmute these energies into pure love and light."

- "Heal and transform any unresolved emotional wounds from past lives that manifest as skin issues in the present. Fill these spaces with radiant light and healing energy."

181

- "I command the full release of any karmic patterns, vows, or agreements from past lives that are affecting my skin in this lifetime. Transmute them into divine perfection."

- "Identify and remove any etheric cords or attachments from past lives that are draining the vitality and health of my skin. Sever these connections and heal the points of origin with divine light."

ADDRESSING PRESENT LIFE SKIN ISSUES

- "Pendulum, connect to all present life experiences and energies related to skin issues."

- "Clear, release, and transmute any emotional, physical, or energetic blockages that are manifesting as skin issues in the present. Replace them with pure love and light."

- "Release any beliefs, thoughts, or feelings of unworthiness, shame, or self-criticism associated with skin issues. Transform these into self-love, acceptance, and confidence."

- "Harmonize all aspects of my life that are contributing to skin issues, bringing balance, peace, and radiant health to my skin."

- "Strengthen the energy flow to my skin, ensuring that it receives all necessary nutrients, oxygen, and life force for optimal health and appearance."

- "Clear any environmental or external influences that are negatively impacting my skin's health. Create a protective shield of light around me to deflect any harmful energies."

ENSURING FUTURE SKIN HEALTH

- "Pendulum, please connect to all future timelines and possibilities related to my skin health."

- "Clear any potential future skin issues before they manifest. Transmute any negative energies into pure love and light."

- "Anchor the energy of radiant, healthy, and beautiful skin into all future timelines. Ensure that my future experiences are filled with praise, compliments, and satisfaction regarding my skin."

- "Strengthen my future self's connection to divine beauty, ensuring that my skin remains vibrant and healthy across all timelines."

- "Plant the seeds of continuous rejuvenation and renewal in all future timelines, allowing my skin to remain youthful and radiant as I age."

- "Establish a lasting energetic blueprint for perfect skin health in all future lifetimes, ensuring that this energy carries forward into every incarnation."

SEAL THE HEALING:

- "I command that all healing done in this session be sealed and protected by divine light, ensuring that it continues to work for my highest good."

- "Close all portals and connections opened during this session, ensuring only positive energies remain."

- "I thank my guides, angels, higher self, and the divine energies for their assistance in this healing session."

- "I am grateful for my radiant, healthy, and beautiful skin. I love and accept myself completely."

HEALING CONCEPT NO: 21

HAIR ISSUES

SET YOUR INTENTION:

- State your intention clearly and firmly: "I intend to address and heal any hair issues from the past, present, and future, transforming them into pure love and light, bringing forth healthy, vibrant, and beautiful hair."

INVOKE DIVINE ASSISTANCE:

- "I call upon the highest divine energies, my guides, angels, and higher self, to assist in this healing session. May this session be for the highest good, in accordance with divine will."

ADDRESSING PAST LIFE HAIR ISSUES

- "Pendulum, please connect to all past life memories, experiences, and energies related to hair issues."

- "Clear and release all past life traumas, scars, and negative imprints associated with hair issues. Transmute these energies into pure love and light."

- "Heal and transform any unresolved emotional wounds from past lives that manifest as hair issues in the present. Fill these spaces with radiant light and healing energy."

- "I command the full release of any karmic patterns, vows, or agreements from past lives that are affecting my hair in this lifetime. Transmute them into divine perfection."

- "Identify and remove any etheric cords or attachments from past lives that are draining the vitality and health of my hair. Sever these connections and heal the points of origin with divine light."

ADDRESSING PRESENT LIFE HAIR ISSUES

- "Pendulum, connect to all present life experiences and energies related to hair issues."

- "Clear, release, and transmute any emotional, physical, or energetic blockages that are manifesting as hair issues in the present. Replace them with pure love and light."

- "Release any beliefs, thoughts, or feelings of unworthiness, shame, or self-criticism associated with hair issues. Transform these into self-love, acceptance, and confidence."

- "Harmonize all aspects of my life that are contributing to hair issues, bringing balance, peace, and vibrant health to my hair."

- "Strengthen the energy flow to my hair follicles, ensuring that they receive all necessary nutrients, oxygen, and life force for optimal growth and health."

○

- "Clear any environmental or external influences that are negatively impacting my hair's health. Create a protective shield of light around me to deflect any harmful energies."

ENSURING FUTURE HAIR HEALTH

- "Pendulum, please connect to all future timelines and possibilities related to my hair health."

- "Clear any potential future hair issues before they manifest. Transmute any negative energies into pure love and light."

- "Anchor the energy of healthy, vibrant, and beautiful hair into all future timelines. Ensure that my future experiences are filled with compliments and satisfaction regarding my hair."

- "Strengthen my future self's connection to divine beauty, ensuring that my hair remains healthy and vibrant across all timelines."

- "Plant the seeds of continuous rejuvenation and renewal in all future timelines, allowing my hair to remain strong and beautiful as I age."

- "Establish a lasting energetic blueprint for perfect hair health in all future lifetimes, ensuring that this energy carries forward into every incarnation."

CLOSING THE SESSION

- "I command that all healing done in this session be sealed and protected by divine light, ensuring that it continues to work for my highest good."

- "Close all portals and connections opened during this session, ensuring only positive energies remain."

- "I thank my guides, angels, higher self, and the divine energies for their assistance in this healing session."

- "I am grateful for my healthy, vibrant, and beautiful hair. I love and accept myself completely."

HEALING CONCEPT NO: 22

WEIGHTLOSS

SET YOUR INTENTION:

- "I intend to address and heal any weight-related issues from the past, present, and future, transforming them into pure love and light, bringing forth a healthy, balanced, and vibrant body."

INVOKE DIVINE ASSISTANCE:

- "I call upon the highest divine energies, my guides, angels, and higher self, to assist in this healing session. May this session be for the highest good, in accordance with divine will."

ADDRESSING PAST LIFE WEIGHT ISSUES

- "Pendulum, please connect to all past life memories, experiences, and energies related to weight issues."

- "Clear and release all past life traumas, beliefs, and negative imprints associated with weight and body image. Transmute these energies into pure love and light."

- "Heal and transform any unresolved emotional wounds from past lives that manifest as weight issues in the present. Fill these spaces with radiant light and healing energy."

- "I command the full release of any karmic patterns, vows, or agreements from past lives that are affecting my weight and body in this lifetime. Transmute them into divine perfection."

- "Identify and remove any etheric cords or attachments from past lives that are connected to body image issues or unhealthy eating patterns. Sever these connections and heal the points of origin with divine light."

ADDRESSING PRESENT LIFE WEIGHT ISSUES

- "Pendulum, connect to all present life experiences and energies related to weight issues."

- "Clear, release, and transmute any emotional, physical, or energetic blockages that are manifesting as weight issues in the present. Replace them with pure love and light."

- "Release any beliefs, thoughts, or feelings of unworthiness, guilt, or self-criticism associated with weight and body image. Transform these into self-love, acceptance, and confidence."

- "Harmonize all aspects of my life that are contributing to weight issues, bringing balance, peace, and vibrant health to my body."

- "Strengthen the energy flow to my metabolism, ensuring that it functions optimally for healthy weight management."

- "Clear any environmental, societal, or external influences that are negatively impacting my body image and weight. Create a protective shield of light around me to deflect any harmful energies."

ENSURING FUTURE WEIGHT AND BODY HEALTH

- "Pendulum, please connect to all future timelines and possibilities related to my weight and body health."

- "Clear any potential future weight issues before they manifest. Transmute any negative energies into pure love and light."

- "Anchor the energy of a healthy, balanced, and vibrant body into all future timelines. Ensure that my future experiences are filled with confidence, self-love, and satisfaction regarding my body."

- "Strengthen my future self's connection to divine health, ensuring that my body remains strong, vibrant, and balanced across all timelines."

- "Plant the seeds of continuous rejuvenation, healthy metabolism, and balanced weight in all future timelines, allowing my body to remain in optimal health as I age."

- "Establish a lasting energetic blueprint for a healthy and balanced body in all future lifetimes, ensuring that this energy carries forward into every incarnation."

CLOSING THE SESSION

- "I command that all healing done in this session be sealed and protected by divine light, ensuring that it continues to work for my highest good."

- "Close all portals and connections opened during this session, ensuring only positive energies remain."

- "I thank my guides, angels, higher self, and the divine energies for their assistance in this healing session."

- "I am grateful for my healthy, balanced, and vibrant body. I love and accept myself completely."

6.

MENTAL HEALING WORKSHEETS

Mental healing is the process of recovering from emotional wounds and restoring psychological well-being. It involves addressing and transforming the thoughts, beliefs, and emotions that contribute to mental distress. As the mind heals, individuals often gain a deeper understanding of themselves, develop healthier coping mechanisms, and cultivate a more positive and balanced outlook on life. Mental healing is essential for achieving emotional resilience, inner peace, and the ability to navigate life's challenges with a clear and focused mind.

HEALING CONCEPT NO: 23

POST TRAUMATIC STRESS DISORDER

SET INTENT:

- "I intend to completely and thoroughly clear all past and future occurrences of PTSD from my energy field, mind, body, and soul, bringing forth lasting peace, healing, and resilience."

CENTERING:

- "I command that my energy be centered and aligned with my highest self. I ask for a protective light to surround and support me throughout this session, ensuring that I remain safe and guided."

CONNECTION TO DIVINE ENERGY:

- "I command an immediate and strong connection to the highest source of divine light, love, and healing energy. I invite my higher self, spiritual guides, ancestors, and any other healing energies aligned with my highest good to assist and support in this session."

- "I command the establishment of a continuous flow of divine energy throughout this session, ensuring that all healing is empowered and magnified by the purest source of light."

IDENTIFYING THE ROOT CAUSES:

- "I command that all root causes of PTSD from this life and all other lives, including hidden, suppressed, or forgotten memories and traumas, be brought to the surface now for full clearing and healing."

- "I command the identification of all ancestral, karmic, and collective influences that have contributed to PTSD, bringing them into awareness to be fully cleared and healed."

CLEARING PAST HISTORY OF PTSD:

- "I command that all traumatic memories, energies, imprints, and patterns contributing to PTSD from all timelines, dimensions, realities, and lives be fully cleared, healed, and transmuted into pure divine light and love. Release all negative patterns, emotions, and energies associated with these traumas now."

- "I command the release and transmutation of any lingering residue, attachments, or energies tied to PTSD from all past lives, ancestral lines, and karmic influences, clearing them completely and permanently to the core."

- "I command that all cellular memory, DNA imprints, emotional body, mental body, and spiritual body be thoroughly cleansed and purified of any PTSD-related energies. Clear all blocks, limitations, and trauma stored in my energy field at all levels."

CLEARING FUTURE OCCURRENCES OF PTSD:

- "I command that any potential future occurrences of PTSD, including triggers, stressors, or situations that may recreate trauma, be neutralized, cleared, and transmuted into pure divine light. Transform these energies into opportunities for peace, healing, and personal growth."

- "I command that my energy field, mind, and soul be fortified with divine protection, ensuring that any future challenges are met with resilience, calm, and inner strength, preventing the reactivation of PTSD in any form."

- "I command that all future timelines where PTSD might occur be healed and aligned with my highest good. Neutralize any negative timelines and align all future possibilities with peace, strength, and healing."

REPLACING WITH POSITIVE ENERGIES:

- "I command that all spaces, memories, and energies cleared of PTSD be filled with divine love, peace, resilience, and healing. I ask that resilience, strength, and a deep sense of safety and empowerment replace all past traumas."

- "I command that these positive energies be anchored deeply into my being, continuously growing, expanding, and strengthening my mind, body, and soul. Let this healing be permanent and self-sustaining."

- "I command that a constant flow of divine love and healing continue to support me daily, ensuring that I remain in a state of peace, empowerment, and well-being."

CLOSING AND GRATITUDE:

- "I command that all the work done in this session be harmonized, balanced, and integrated into my entire being, across all levels and layers of consciousness, with ease, grace, and completeness."

- "I command the integration of all healing at the cellular level, ensuring that every cell in my body, every thought, and every emotion resonates with peace, resilience, and divine love."

- "I close this healing session, thanking all the divine energies, guides, and my higher self for their assistance. I seal this work with love, light, and gratitude, ensuring that the healing continues to unfold in the most perfect way."

- "I command that this healing be sealed with a protective layer of divine light, ensuring that only positive, loving energies remain within and around me, and that this healing is protected and permanent."

- "I command the expression of deep gratitude to all energies and beings that have assisted in this session. I honor their presence and the healing that has taken place."

- "I now ground myself back into the present moment, fully aware, balanced, and centered. I command that I remain grounded, clear, and connected to the earth as I integrate this healing."

- "I command that my energy be stabilized and balanced, ensuring that I feel secure, empowered, and centered moving forward."

HEALING CONCEPT NO: 24

OBSESSIVE COMPULSIVE DISORDER

OBJECTIVE:

- To clear all past history and future occurrences of Obsessive-Compulsive Disorder (OCD), transforming obsessive patterns into peace, balance, and freedom.

SET INTENT:

- "I intend to completely and thoroughly clear all past and future occurrences of OCD from my energy field, mind, body, and soul, bringing forth lasting peace, balance, and freedom."

CENTERING:

- "I command that my energy be centered and aligned with my highest self. I ask for a protective light to surround and support me throughout this session, ensuring that I remain safe and guided."

CONNECTION TO DIVINE ENERGY:

- "I command an immediate and strong connection to the highest source of divine light, love, and healing energy. I invite my higher self, spiritual guides, ancestors, and any other healing energies aligned with my highest good to assist and support in this session."

- "I command the establishment of a continuous flow of divine energy throughout this session, ensuring that all healing is empowered and magnified by the purest source of light."

IDENTIFYING THE ROOT CAUSES:

- "I command that all root causes of OCD from this life and all other lives, including hidden, suppressed, or forgotten patterns and influences, be brought to the surface now for full clearing and healing."

- "I command the identification of all ancestral, karmic, and collective influences that have contributed to OCD, bringing them into awareness to be fully cleared and healed."

CLEARING PAST HISTORY OF OCD:

- "I command that all obsessive thoughts, behaviors, patterns, and energies contributing to OCD from all timelines, dimensions, realities, and lives be fully cleared, healed, and transmuted into pure divine light and love. Release all negative patterns, emotions, and energies associated with these compulsions now."

- "I command the release and transmutation of any lingering residue, attachments, or energies tied to OCD from all past lives, ancestral lines, and karmic influences, clearing them completely and permanently to the core."

- "I command that all cellular memory, DNA imprints, emotional body, mental body, and spiritual body be thoroughly cleansed and purified of any OCD-related energies. Clear all blocks, limitations, and patterns stored in my energy field at all levels."

CLEARING FUTURE OCCURRENCES OF OCD:

- "I command that any potential future occurrences of OCD, including triggers, stressors, or situations that may recreate obsessive patterns, be neutralized, cleared, and transmuted into pure divine light. Transform these energies into opportunities for peace, balance, and freedom."

- "I command that my energy field, mind, and soul be fortified with divine protection, ensuring that any future challenges are met with calmness, clarity, and inner peace, preventing the reactivation of OCD in any form."

- "I command that all future timelines where OCD might occur be healed and aligned with my highest good. Neutralize any negative timelines and align all future possibilities with peace, balance, and freedom."

REPLACING WITH POSITIVE ENERGIES:

- "I command that all spaces, memories, and energies cleared of OCD be filled with divine love, peace, clarity, and balance. I ask that freedom, inner peace, and a deep sense of calm replace all past obsessions."

- "I command that these positive energies be anchored deeply into my being, continuously growing, expanding, and strengthening my mind, body, and soul. Let this healing be permanent and self-sustaining."

- "I command that a constant flow of divine love and healing continue to support me daily, ensuring that I remain in a state of peace, balance, and freedom."

CLOSING AND INTEGRATING:

- "I command that all the work done in this session be harmonized, balanced, and integrated into my entire being, across all levels and layers of consciousness, with ease, grace, and completeness."

- "I command the integration of all healing at the cellular level, ensuring that every cell in my body, every thought, and every emotion resonates with peace, balance, and divine love."

- "I close this healing session, thanking all the divine energies, guides, and my higher self for their assistance. I seal this work with love, light, and gratitude, ensuring that the healing continues to unfold in the most perfect way."

- "I command that this healing be sealed with a protective layer of divine light, ensuring that only positive, loving energies remain within and around me, and that this healing is protected and permanent."

- "I command the expression of deep gratitude to all energies and beings that have assisted in this session. I honor their presence and the healing that has taken place."

- "I now ground myself back into the present moment, fully aware, balanced, and centered. I command that I remain grounded, clear, and connected to the earth as I integrate this healing."

- "I command that my energy be stabilized and balanced, ensuring that I feel secure, empowered, and centered moving forward."

HEALING SESSION NO: 25

PHOBIAS

OBJECTIVE:

- To clear all past history and future occurrences of phobias, transforming fear into peace, courage, and confidence.

SET INTENT:

- "I intend to completely and thoroughly clear all past and future occurrences of phobias from my energy field, mind, body, and soul, replacing fear with lasting peace, courage, and confidence."

CENTERING:

- "I command that my energy be centered and aligned with my highest self. I ask for a protective light to surround and support me throughout this session, ensuring that I remain safe and guided."

CONNECTION TO DIVINE ENERGY:

- "I command an immediate and strong connection to the highest source of divine light, love, and healing energy. I invite my higher self, spiritual guides, ancestors, and any other healing energies aligned with my highest good to assist and support in this session."

- "I command the establishment of a continuous flow of divine energy throughout this session, ensuring that all healing is empowered and magnified by the purest source of light."

IDENTIFYING THE ROOT CAUSES:

- "I command that all root causes of phobias from this life and all other lives, including hidden, suppressed, or forgotten fears and traumas, be brought to the surface now for full clearing and healing."

- "I command the identification of all ancestral, karmic, and collective influences that have contributed to phobias, bringing them into awareness to be fully cleared and healed."

CLEARING PAST HISTORY OF PHOBIAS:

- "I command that all fearful thoughts, emotions, memories, and energies contributing to phobias from all timelines, dimensions, realities, and lives be fully cleared, healed, and transmuted into pure divine light and love. Release all negative patterns, emotions, and energies associated with these fears now."

- "I command the release and transmutation of any lingering residue, attachments, or energies tied to phobias from all past lives, ancestral lines, and karmic influences, clearing them completely and permanently to the core."

- "I command that all cellular memory, DNA imprints, emotional body, mental body, and spiritual body be thoroughly cleansed and purified of any phobia-related energies. Clear all blocks, limitations, and patterns stored in my energy field at all levels."

CLEARING FUTURE OCCURRENCES OF PHOBIAS:

- "I command that any potential future occurrences of phobias, including triggers, stressors, or situations that may recreate fears, be neutralized, cleared, and transmuted into pure divine light. Transform these energies into opportunities for peace, courage, and confidence."

- "I command that my energy field, mind, and soul be fortified with divine protection, ensuring that any future challenges are met with calmness, bravery, and inner strength, preventing the reactivation of phobias in any form."

- "I command that all future timelines where phobias might occur be healed and aligned with my highest good. Neutralize any negative timelines and align all future possibilities with peace, courage, and confidence."

HEALING AND REPLACING WITH POSITIVE ENERGIES:

- "I command that all spaces, memories, and energies cleared of phobias be filled with divine love, peace, bravery, and confidence. I ask that courage, inner strength, and a deep sense of calm replace all past fears."

- "I command that these positive energies be anchored deeply into my being, continuously growing, expanding, and strengthening my mind, body, and soul. Let this healing be permanent and self-sustaining."

- "I command that a constant flow of divine love and healing continue to support me daily, ensuring that I remain in a state of peace, bravery, and confidence."

CLOSING AND INTEGRATING:

- "I command that all the work done in this session be harmonized, balanced, and integrated into my entire being, across all levels and layers of consciousness, with ease, grace, and completeness."

- "I command the integration of all healing at the cellular level, ensuring that every cell in my body, every thought, and every emotion resonates with peace, courage, and divine love."

- "I close this healing session, thanking all the divine energies, guides, and my higher self for their assistance. I seal this work with love, light, and gratitude, ensuring that the healing continues to unfold in the most perfect way."

- "I command that this healing be sealed with a protective layer of divine light, ensuring that only positive, loving energies remain within and around me, and that this healing is protected and permanent."

- "I command the expression of deep gratitude to all energies and beings that have assisted in this session. I honor their presence and the healing that has taken place."

- "I now ground myself back into the present moment, fully aware, balanced, and centered. I command that I remain grounded, clear, and connected to the earth as I integrate this healing."

- "I command that my energy be stabilized and balanced, ensuring that I feel secure, empowered, and centered moving forward."

HEALING SESSION NO: 26

TOXIC ADDICTIONS

OBJECTIVE:

- To clear all past history and future occurrences of toxic addictions, transforming addiction into freedom, self-control, and healthy choices.

SET INTENT:

- "I intend to completely and thoroughly clear all past and future occurrences of toxic addictions from my energy field, mind, body, and soul, replacing addiction with lasting freedom, self-control, and healthy choices."

CENTERING:

- "I command that my energy be centered and aligned with my highest self. I ask for a protective light to surround and support me throughout this session, ensuring that I remain safe and guided."

CONNECTION TO DIVINE ENERGY:

- "I command an immediate and strong connection to the highest source of divine light, love, and healing energy. I invite my higher self, spiritual guides, ancestors, and any other healing energies aligned with my highest good to assist and support in this session."

- "I command the establishment of a continuous flow of divine energy throughout this session, ensuring that all healing is empowered and magnified by the purest source of light."

IDENTIFYING THE ROOT CAUSES:

- "I command that all root causes of toxic addictions from this life and all other lives, including hidden, suppressed, or forgotten influences and traumas, be brought to the surface now for full clearing and healing."

- "I command the identification of all ancestral, karmic, and collective influences that have contributed to toxic addictions, bringing them into awareness to be fully cleared and healed."

CLEARING PAST HISTORY OF TOXIC ADDICTIONS:

- "I command that all addictive thoughts, behaviors, cravings, and energies contributing to toxic addictions from all timelines, dimensions, realities, and lives be fully cleared, healed, and transmuted into pure divine light and love. Release all negative patterns, emotions, and energies associated with these addictions now."

- "I command the release and transmutation of any lingering residue, attachments, or energies tied to toxic addictions from all past lives, ancestral lines, and karmic influences, clearing them completely and permanently to the core."

- "I command that all cellular memory, DNA imprints, emotional body, mental body, and spiritual body be thoroughly cleansed and purified of any addiction-related energies. Clear all blocks, limitations, and patterns stored in my energy field at all levels."

CLEARING FUTURE OCCURRENCES OF TOXIC ADDICTIONS:

- "I command that any potential future occurrences of toxic addictions, including triggers, stressors, or situations that may recreate cravings or addictive behaviors, be neutralized, cleared, and transmuted into pure divine light. Transform these energies into opportunities for freedom, self-control, and healthy choices."

- "I command that my energy field, mind, and soul be fortified with divine protection, ensuring that any future challenges are met with strength, clarity, and inner peace, preventing the reactivation of toxic addictions in any form."

- "I command that all future timelines where toxic addictions might occur be healed and aligned with my highest good. Neutralize any negative timelines and align all future possibilities with freedom, self-control, and healthy choices."

HEALING AND REPLACING WITH POSITIVE ENERGIES:

- "I command that all spaces, memories, and energies cleared of toxic addictions be filled with divine love, freedom, self-control, and healthy habits. I ask that inner strength, resilience, and a deep sense of well-being replace all past addictions."

- "I command that these positive energies be anchored deeply into my being, continuously growing, expanding, and strengthening my mind, body, and soul. Let this healing be permanent and self-sustaining."

- "I command that a constant flow of divine love and healing continue to support me daily, ensuring that I remain in a state of freedom, self-control, and healthy choices."

HARMONIZING AND INTEGRATING:

- "I command that all the work done in this session be harmonized, balanced, and integrated into my entire being, across all levels and layers of consciousness, with ease, grace, and completeness."

- "I command the integration of all healing at the cellular level, ensuring that every cell in my body, every thought, and every emotion resonates with freedom, self-control, and divine love."

CLOSING AND GRATITUDE:

- "I close this healing session, thanking all the divine energies, guides, and my higher self for their assistance. I seal this work with love, light, and gratitude, ensuring that the healing continues to unfold in the most perfect way."

- "I command that this healing be sealed with a protective layer of divine light, ensuring that only positive, loving energies remain within and around me, and that this healing is protected and permanent."

- "I command the expression of deep gratitude to all energies and beings that have assisted in this session. I honor their presence and the healing that has taken place."

GROUNDING:

- "I now ground myself back into the present moment, fully aware, balanced, and centered. I command that I remain grounded, clear, and connected to the earth as I integrate this healing."

- "I command that my energy be stabilized and balanced, ensuring that I feel secure, empowered, and centered moving forward."

7.

ENERGY NURTURING WORKSHEETS

Emotional healing is the process of recovering from deep-seated emotional pain and restoring a sense of inner peace and balance. It involves acknowledging and understanding the emotions that have been suppressed or unresolved, and gradually working through them to find closure and release. As emotional healing progresses, it brings about a renewed sense of clarity, self-acceptance, and emotional freedom, allowing you to move forward with greater resilience and a more open heart. It's about reclaiming your emotional well-being and embracing life with a lighter, more empowered spirit.

HEALING CONCEPT NO: 27
RESENTMENT AND ANGER

INTENTION SETTING

- "I intend to release all anger and resentment from the point of birth and transform these energies into love, peace, and harmony."

CLEARING ANGER AND RESENTMENT FROM BIRTH

- "I command to clear, release, and transmute all anger and resentment from the moment of my birth, in all dimensions, lifetimes, and realities, back to the source."

- "I command to neutralize and dissolve any energetic imprints or memories of anger and resentment held in my cells, DNA, and energy field."

Hold the pendulum over your heart chakra and let it spin. Visualize a bright white light entering your body, focusing on releasing any stored anger and resentment. Allow the pendulum to move until it stops or changes direction, indicating that the energy has been cleared.

RELEASING ALL PATTERNS AND REACTIONS

- "I command to clear, release, and transmute all patterns, reactions, and triggers related to anger and resentment, across all timelines, dimensions, and realities."

- "I command to dissolve all karmic contracts, vows, and agreements that perpetuate anger and resentment in my life, across all incarnations."

Move the pendulum over your solar plexus chakra. Visualize any negative patterns or reactions dissolving into light. Let the pendulum spin until the clearing is complete.

HEALING AND TRANSFORMING THE ENERGY

- "I command to fill the space once occupied by anger and resentment with pure love, peace, and compassion, in all dimensions, lifetimes, and realities."

- "I command to restore my emotional body to its natural state of balance and harmony, free from the influence of anger and resentment."

Move the pendulum over your heart and crown chakras, visualizing them filling with soft, loving light. Allow the pendulum to move until it naturally comes to a stop.

REPROGRAMMING THE MIND

- "I command to reprogram my subconscious mind with thoughts, beliefs, and patterns of peace, forgiveness, and unconditional love."

- "I command to replace all negative thought forms and mental patterns related to anger and resentment with empowering and loving affirmations."

Hold the pendulum over your third eye chakra, visualizing your mind being filled with positive, loving thoughts. Allow the pendulum to move until the reprogramming is complete.

SEALING THE HEALING

- "I command to seal this healing with unconditional love and divine protection, ensuring that the energies released do not return, and that only love, peace, and harmony remain."

- "I command to create a protective shield of light around my energy field, repelling any external influences of anger or resentment."

Hold the pendulum over your heart chakra once more, visualizing a protective light surrounding you, sealing in the healing work done.

HEALING SESSION NO: 28
SELF CARE

INTENTION SETTING:

- "I intend to enhance my self-care practices, fully embracing self-love, nurturing, and the consistent care of my physical, emotional, and spiritual well-being."

CLEARING BLOCKS TO SELF-CARE

- "I command to clear, release, and transmute all blocks, resistance, and limiting beliefs preventing me from fully embracing self-care, across all timelines, dimensions, and realities."

- "I command to dissolve any guilt, shame, or fear associated with prioritizing my self-care."

Hold the pendulum over your heart chakra and let it spin. Visualize a bright white light entering your body, clearing away any obstacles to self-care. Allow the pendulum to move until the clearing is complete.

ENHANCING SELF-LOVE AND NURTURING

- "I command to activate and enhance my ability to love and nurture myself unconditionally, treating myself with kindness, compassion, and respect."

- "I command to awaken and amplify my natural instincts for self-care, ensuring I consistently meet my physical, emotional, and spiritual needs."

Move the pendulum over your heart and sacral chakras, visualizing these areas filling with soft, nurturing light. Let the pendulum spin until the energy is fully activated.

REINFORCING POSITIVE SELF-CARE HABITS

- "I command to reprogram my subconscious mind with positive self-care habits and routines that support my overall well-being."

- "I command to instill a deep sense of worthiness and deservingness within me, so that I naturally prioritize my self-care."

Hold the pendulum over your solar plexus chakra, visualizing yourself engaging in daily self-care practices with joy and ease. Allow the pendulum to move until the new habits are reinforced.

CONNECTING WITH INNER GUIDANCE

- "I command to strengthen my connection with my inner guidance, so I can intuitively know what self-care practices are best for me at any given time."

- "I command to open and align my intuition with my self-care needs, ensuring I respond promptly and effectively to what my body, mind, and spirit require."

Move the pendulum over your third eye chakra, visualizing your intuition guiding you toward the best self-care practices for you. Let the pendulum spin until the connection is solidified.

SEALING THE HEALING

- "I command to seal this healing with unconditional love and divine protection, ensuring that my commitment to self-care remains strong and unwavering."

- "I command to create a protective shield of light around my energy field, supporting my ongoing dedication to self-care and nurturing."

Hold the pendulum over your heart chakra once more, visualizing a protective light surrounding you, sealing in the healing work done.

HEALING CONCEPT NO: 29
SELF WORTH

INTENTION SETTING:

- "I intend to enhance my self-worth, fully embracing my inherent value, and recognizing my worthiness of love, respect, and success."

CLEARING BLOCKS TO SELF-WORTH

- "I command to clear, release, and transmute all blocks, resistance, and limiting beliefs that diminish my sense of self-worth, across all timelines, dimensions, and realities."

- "I command to dissolve any feelings of unworthiness, self-doubt, or inadequacy, freeing myself from these negative patterns."

Hold the pendulum over your heart chakra and let it spin. Visualize a bright white light entering your body, clearing away any obstacles to recognizing your self-worth. Allow the pendulum to move until the clearing is complete.

HEALING PAST WOUNDS

- "I command to heal and release any past experiences, traumas, or relationships that have contributed to a diminished sense of self-worth."

- "I command to forgive myself and others for any actions, words, or situations that have led to feelings of unworthiness."

Move the pendulum over your solar plexus chakra, visualizing healing light filling any wounds or scars from past experiences. Let the pendulum spin until the healing is complete.

ACTIVATING AND ENHANCING SELF-WORTH

- "I command to activate and amplify my inherent self-worth, allowing me to fully recognize and embrace my value and deservingness of all good things."

- "I command to strengthen my inner confidence and self-belief, empowering me to take actions that reflect my true worth."

Move the pendulum over your heart and solar plexus chakras, visualizing them filling with radiant, golden light, representing your self-worth shining brightly. Allow the pendulum to move until the energy is fully activated.

REPROGRAMMING THE MIND

- "I command to reprogram my subconscious mind with positive beliefs and affirmations that support and enhance my self-worth."

- "I command to replace all negative self-talk and limiting beliefs with thoughts and patterns that reflect my true value and worthiness."

Hold the pendulum over your third eye chakra, visualizing your mind being filled with empowering and affirming thoughts about your worth. Allow the pendulum to move until the reprogramming is complete.

SEALING THE HEALING

- "I command to seal this healing with unconditional love and divine protection, ensuring that my sense of self-worth remains strong and unshakable."

- "I command to create a protective shield of light around my energy field, supporting my ongoing recognition and embodiment of my self-worth."

Hold the pendulum over your heart chakra once more, visualizing a protective light surrounding you, sealing in the healing work done.

HEALING CONCEPT NO: 30

I AM GOOD ENOUGH

INTENTION SETTING:

- "I intend to fully embrace the belief that I am good enough, releasing all doubts and insecurities, and embodying my true worth and potential."

CLEARING DOUBTS AND INSECURITIES

- "I command to clear, release, and transmute all doubts, insecurities, and feelings of inadequacy that prevent me from believing I am good enough, across all timelines, dimensions, and realities."

- "I command to dissolve any external influences, criticisms, or negative experiences that have led me to question my worthiness."

Hold the pendulum over your solar plexus chakra and let it spin. Visualize a bright white light entering your body, clearing away any doubts or insecurities. Allow the pendulum to move until the clearing is complete.

HEALING PAST EXPERIENCES

- "I command to heal and release any past experiences or traumas that have contributed to feelings of not being good enough."

- "I command to forgive myself and others for any actions, words, or situations that have reinforced these negative beliefs."

Move the pendulum over your heart chakra, visualizing healing light filling any wounds or scars from past experiences. Let the pendulum spin until the healing is complete.

EMBRACING THE AFFIRMATION "I AM GOOD ENOUGH"

- "I command to activate and fully integrate the belief that I am good enough, exactly as I am, in every aspect of my life."

- "I command to align my thoughts, feelings, and actions with the affirmation 'I am good enough,' allowing it to become a core part of my identity."

Move the pendulum over your heart and solar plexus chakras, visualizing them filling with golden light, symbolizing your acceptance of being good enough. Allow the pendulum to move until the energy is fully activated.

REPROGRAMMING THE MIND

- "I command to reprogram my subconscious mind with the affirmation 'I am good enough,' reinforcing this belief in every cell of my being."

- "I command to replace all negative self-talk and limiting beliefs with the empowering affirmation 'I am good enough' in all situations."

Hold the pendulum over your third eye chakra, visualizing your mind being filled with the affirmation 'I am good enough' repeatedly. Allow the pendulum to move until the reprogramming is complete.

SEALING THE HEALING

- "I command to seal this healing with unconditional love and divine protection, ensuring that my belief in being good enough remains strong and unwavering."

- "I command to create a protective shield of light around my energy field, supporting my ongoing embodiment of the affirmation 'I am good enough.'"

Hold the pendulum over your heart chakra once more, visualizing a protective light surrounding you, sealing in the healing work done.

HEALING SESSION NO: 31
SELF LOVE AND ACCEPTANCE

INTENTION SETTING:

- "I intend to fully cultivate self-love and acceptance, embracing myself wholly and unconditionally."

CLEARING BLOCKS TO SELF-LOVE AND ACCEPTANCE

- "I command to clear, release, and transmute all blocks, resistance, and limiting beliefs preventing me from fully loving and accepting myself, across all timelines, dimensions, and realities."

- "I command to dissolve any feelings of self-judgment, criticism, or unworthiness that hinder my ability to embrace self-love and acceptance."

Hold the pendulum over your heart chakra and let it spin. Visualize a bright white light entering your body, clearing away any obstacles to self-love and acceptance. Allow the pendulum to move until the clearing is complete.

HEALING PAST WOUNDS

- "I command to heal and release any past experiences, traumas, or relationships that have contributed to feelings of unworthiness, self-rejection, or a lack of self-love."

- "I command to forgive myself and others for any actions, words, or situations that have led to a diminished sense of self-worth."

Move the pendulum over your solar plexus chakra, visualizing healing light filling any wounds or scars from past experiences. Let the pendulum spin until the healing is complete.

ACTIVATING AND ENHANCING SELF-LOVE

- "I command to activate and amplify my ability to love and accept myself unconditionally, embracing all aspects of who I am."

- "I command to align my thoughts, feelings, and actions with the energy of self-love, ensuring that I consistently honor and care for myself."

Move the pendulum over your heart and sacral chakras, visualizing them filling with soft, pink or golden light, symbolizing unconditional love and acceptance. Allow the pendulum to move until the energy is fully activated.

REPROGRAMMING THE MIND

- "I command to reprogram my subconscious mind with positive affirmations of self-love and acceptance, reinforcing these beliefs in every cell of my being."

- "I command to replace all negative self-talk and limiting beliefs with loving and accepting thoughts about myself."

Hold the pendulum over your third eye chakra, visualizing your mind being filled with loving, supportive thoughts about yourself. Allow the pendulum to move until the reprogramming is complete.

SEALING THE HEALING

- "I command to seal this healing with unconditional love and divine protection, ensuring that my sense of self-love and acceptance remains strong and unwavering."

- "I command to create a protective shield of light around my energy field, supporting my ongoing cultivation of self-love and acceptance."

Hold the pendulum over your heart chakra once more, visualizing a protective light surrounding you, sealing in the healing work done.

HEALING SESSION NO 32

SELF FORGIVENESS AND COMPASSION

INTENTION SETTING:

- "I intend to fully cultivate self-forgiveness and compassion, releasing any burdens of guilt and shame, and embracing myself with kindness and understanding."

CLEARING GUILT AND SHAME

- "I command to clear, release, and transmute all feelings of guilt, shame, and regret that prevent me from forgiving myself, across all timelines, dimensions, and realities."

- "I command to dissolve any negative self-judgment and criticism that have rooted in my energy field, keeping me from experiencing self-compassion."

Hold the pendulum over your solar plexus chakra and let it spin. Visualize a bright white light entering your body, clearing away any energies of guilt and shame. Allow the pendulum to move until the clearing is complete.

HEALING PAST WOUNDS

- "I command to heal and release any past experiences, actions, or decisions that I have not forgiven myself for, allowing these wounds to be transformed into wisdom and understanding."

- "I command to forgive myself completely and unconditionally, releasing all burdens of the past and embracing peace within myself."

Move the pendulum over your heart chakra, visualizing healing light filling any areas where guilt or regret have left an imprint. Let the pendulum spin until the healing is complete.

ACTIVATING SELF-FORGIVENESS AND COMPASSION

- "I command to activate and amplify my ability to forgive myself fully and to treat myself with compassion and kindness in all situations."

- "I command to align my thoughts, feelings, and actions with the energy of self-forgiveness and compassion, ensuring that I nurture myself with love and understanding."

Move the pendulum over your heart and sacral chakras, visualizing them filling with soft, pink or golden light, symbolizing deep compassion and forgiveness. Allow the pendulum to move until the energy is fully activated.

REPROGRAMMING THE MIND

- "I command to reprogram my subconscious mind with positive affirmations of self-forgiveness and compassion, reinforcing these beliefs in every cell of my being."

- "I command to replace all negative self-talk and critical thoughts with loving, forgiving, and compassionate thoughts toward myself."

Hold the pendulum over your third eye chakra, visualizing your mind being filled with affirmations of forgiveness and compassion. Allow the pendulum to move until the reprogramming is complete.

SEALING THE HEALING

- "I command to seal this healing with unconditional love and divine protection, ensuring that my ability to forgive myself and show compassion remains strong and unwavering."

- "I command to create a protective shield of light around my energy field, supporting my ongoing journey of self-forgiveness and compassion."

Hold the pendulum over your heart chakra once more, visualizing a protective light surrounding you, sealing in the healing work done.

PART 4:

SPIRITUAL HEALING

8.

SOUL FRAGMENTATION WORKSHEETS

Soul fragmentation refers to the experience of losing parts of one's inner essence or energy, often as a result of trauma, intense stress, or emotional pain. When we go through deeply challenging experiences, it can feel as though pieces of our soul, or core self, become disconnected or lost, leading to a sense of emptiness, disconnection, or feeling incomplete. This fragmentation can manifest as persistent feelings of unease, a lack of wholeness, or difficulty in fully engaging with life. Healing soul fragmentation involves a journey of reclaiming these lost parts, often through practices like soul retrieval, meditation, or deep emotional healing, to restore a sense of wholeness and reconnect with one's true essence.

HEALING SESSION NO: 33

PAST LIFE RECONCILIATION

OBJECTIVE:

- To reconcile past life energies, release lingering attachments, and integrate the lessons learned into the present life for spiritual growth and healing.

INTENTION SETTING:

- "I intend to reconcile any unresolved energies from my past lives, release what no longer serves me, and integrate the wisdom gained into my present life for my highest good."

GROUNDING AND PROTECTION

- "I command to ground myself deeply into the Earth's energy, feeling stable and secure."

- "I command to anchor my energy firmly into the Earth's core, drawing strength and stability from its center."

- "I call upon divine protection, surrounding myself with pure white light, shielding me from any lower energies or influences."

- "I command the formation of a protective barrier around my energy field, filtering only love and light."

Visualize roots growing from your feet into the Earth, anchoring you. Envision a bubble of white light surrounding you, keeping you safe and protected.

CONNECTION WITH HIGHER SELF AND SPIRITUAL GUIDES

- "I command to connect with my Higher Self and spiritual guides who are here to assist me in this healing session."

- "I command to strengthen my connection with divine wisdom, ensuring clarity and accuracy in the information received."

- "I ask my Higher Self to reveal the most important past life that needs reconciliation at this time."

- "I command to open a clear channel of communication with my spiritual guides, receiving their guidance with ease and grace."

Take a moment to feel or sense the presence of your Higher Self and guides. Trust that they are guiding you through this process.

IDENTIFICATION OF PAST LIFE ISSUES

- "I command to bring forth the memories, emotions, and lessons from the identified past life that require healing and reconciliation."

- "I command to uncover any hidden or suppressed energies from this past life that may be affecting my current life."

- "I ask my Higher Self to show me the connections between this past life and my current life challenges or patterns."

- "I command to reveal any unresolved karmic ties or contracts that need to be addressed and released."

Allow any images, feelings, or thoughts to surface. You may receive these insights through your intuition, visions, or emotions.

RELEASE AND RECONCILIATION

- "I command to release any negative emotions, attachments, or karmic ties that are connected to this past life."

- "I command to dissolve any lingering energetic cords or ties with individuals, places, or events from this past life."

- "I command to transmute any unresolved conflicts or traumas from this past life into pure love and light."

- "I command to reconcile and integrate the lessons learned from this past life, transmuting any remaining energies into pure love and light."

- "I command to release all vows, oaths, and contracts from this past life that no longer serve my highest good."

Visualize a gentle release of any heavy or dark energies. Imagine these energies transforming into light and merging back into your being, bringing peace and wisdom.

HEALING AND INTEGRATION

- "I command to heal any wounds or traumas associated with this past life, restoring harmony and balance within my soul."

- "I command to mend any fragmented parts of my soul, bringing them back into wholeness and unity."

- "I command to integrate the wisdom and positive qualities from this past life into my current life, enhancing my spiritual growth and evolution."

- "I command to realign my energy field, ensuring that all aspects of my being are in perfect harmony with my present life's purpose."

- "I command to activate any dormant talents, abilities, or gifts from this past life that are beneficial to my current life."

Feel the healing energy flow through you, mending any broken or fragmented parts of your soul. Imagine yourself absorbing the knowledge and strength gained from this experience.

BALANCING AND HARMONIZATION

- "I command to balance and harmonize all energies within my body, mind, and spirit, ensuring alignment with my highest self."

- "I command to restore the natural flow of energy within my chakras, clearing any blockages related to this past life."

- "I command to harmonize my present life with the healed aspects of my past life, ensuring a smooth and effortless integration."

- "I command to anchor this new state of balance and harmony into my daily life, allowing it to manifest in all areas of my experience."

Visualize your energy centers glowing brightly and spinning freely, in perfect alignment with each other. Feel the sense of peace and balance settle into your being.

GRATITUDE AND CLOSING

- "I express deep gratitude to my Higher Self, spiritual guides, and the divine for their support and guidance during this healing session."

- "I command to close this session, sealing the healing and integration process with love and light."

- "I command to lock in all the positive shifts and transformations that have occurred during this session, ensuring they are permanent and lasting."

- "I command to gently disconnect from any energies or entities that are no longer needed, with gratitude and respect."

Take a moment to feel the completion of the session. Express your thanks and gently bring your awareness back to the present moment.

HEALING SESSION NO: 34

SOUL RETRIEVAL

OBJECTIVE:

- To retrieve lost or fragmented parts of the soul that may have been separated due to trauma, life challenges, or past life experiences. The goal is to restore wholeness, balance, and harmony within the soul.

INTENTION SETTING:

- "I intend to retrieve and reintegrate all fragmented parts of my soul, restoring my wholeness and alignment with my true self."

GROUNDING AND PROTECTION

- "I command to ground myself deeply into the Earth's energy, feeling stable and secure."

- "I command to anchor my energy firmly into the Earth's core, drawing strength and stability from its center."

- "I call upon divine protection, surrounding myself with pure white light, shielding me from any lower energies or influences."

- "I command to establish a protective barrier around my energy field, filtering only love and light."

Visualize roots growing from your feet into the Earth, anchoring you. Envision a bubble of white light surrounding you, keeping you safe and protected.

CONNECTION WITH HIGHER SELF AND SPIRITUAL GUIDES

- "I command to connect with my Higher Self and spiritual guides who are here to assist me in this healing session."

- "I command to strengthen my connection with divine wisdom, ensuring clarity and accuracy in the information received."

- "I command to call forth any lost or fragmented parts of my soul that are ready to be retrieved and reintegrated."

- "I command to open a clear channel of communication with my spiritual guides, receiving their guidance with ease and grace."

Feel the presence of your Higher Self and guides, trusting their support throughout the session.

IDENTIFICATION OF FRAGMENTED SOUL PARTS

- "I command to identify any lost or fragmented parts of my soul, whether from this life, past lives, or other dimensions."

- "I command to bring forth the memories, emotions, and circumstances surrounding the fragmentation of these soul parts."

- "I command to reveal any unresolved traumas, fears, or attachments that may be holding these soul parts in separation."

- "I command to understand the connections between these fragmented soul parts and my current life challenges or patterns."

Allow any images, feelings, or thoughts to surface. These insights may come through intuition, visions, or emotions.

RETRIEVAL AND RECONNECTION

- "I command to retrieve all lost or fragmented parts of my soul, bringing them back to their rightful place within my being."

- "I command to dissolve any barriers, blocks, or resistance preventing the reintegration of these soul parts."

- "I command to heal and restore the connection between these soul parts and the core essence of my being."

- "I command to release any negative energies, attachments, or entities that may be associated with these soul fragments."

- "I command to transmute all energies surrounding these soul parts into pure love and light, ensuring their safe and harmonious return."

Visualize the lost or fragmented parts of your soul returning to you, merging back into your energy field, and bringing with them a sense of wholeness and completeness.

HEALING AND REINTEGRATION

- "I command to heal any wounds or traumas associated with the fragmentation of my soul, restoring harmony and balance within my being."

- "I command to integrate these retrieved soul parts fully, ensuring that they are aligned with my present life's purpose."

- "I command to restore my soul's integrity, bringing all aspects of my being into perfect unity and coherence."

- "I command to activate the strengths, gifts, and wisdom that these soul parts carry, enhancing my spiritual growth and evolution."

- "I command to harmonize my energy field, ensuring that all retrieved parts are fully integrated and functioning in alignment with my highest self."

Feel the healing energy flow through you, mending any broken or fragmented parts of your soul. Imagine yourself absorbing the knowledge and strength gained from this experience.

BALANCING AND HARMONIZATION

- "I command to balance and harmonize all energies within my body, mind, and spirit, ensuring alignment with my highest self."

- "I command to restore the natural flow of energy within my chakras, clearing any blockages related to the fragmentation of my soul."

- "I command to harmonize my present life with the retrieved aspects of my soul, ensuring a smooth and effortless integration."

- "I command to anchor this new state of balance and harmony into my daily life, allowing it to manifest in all areas of my experience."

Visualize your energy centers glowing brightly and spinning freely, in perfect alignment with each other. Feel the sense of peace and balance settle into your being.

GRATITUDE AND CLOSING

- "I express deep gratitude to my Higher Self, spiritual guides, and the divine for their support and guidance during this healing session."

- "I command to close this session, sealing the healing and integration process with love and light."

- "I command to lock in all the positive shifts and transformations that have occurred during this session, ensuring they are permanent and lasting."

- "I command to gently disconnect from any energies or entities that are no longer needed, with gratitude and respect."

Take a moment to feel the completion of the session. Express your thanks and gently bring your awareness back to the present moment.

HEALING SESSION NO: 35
ENERGY RETRIEVAL

OBJECTIVE:

- To retrieve lost or scattered energy that may have been drained, fragmented, or left behind in various situations, relationships, or life events. The goal is to restore vitality, strength, and a sense of completeness within your energy field.

INTENTION SETTING:

- "I intend to retrieve all lost, scattered, or drained energy, restoring my vitality and aligning with my highest self."

GROUNDING AND PROTECTION

- "I command to ground myself deeply into the Earth's energy, feeling stable and secure."

- "I command to anchor my energy firmly into the Earth's core, drawing strength and stability from its center."

- "I call upon divine protection, surrounding myself with pure white light, shielding me from any lower energies or influences."

- "I command to establish a protective barrier around my energy field, filtering only love and light."

Visualize roots growing from your feet into the Earth, anchoring you. Envision a bubble of white light surrounding you, keeping you safe and protected.

CONNECTION WITH HIGHER SELF AND SPIRITUAL GUIDES

- "I command to connect with my Higher Self and spiritual guides who are here to assist me in this healing session."

- "I command to strengthen my connection with divine wisdom, ensuring clarity and accuracy in the information received."

- "I command to call forth all energy that has been lost, scattered, or drained, and that is ready to be retrieved and reintegrated."

- "I command to open a clear channel of communication with my spiritual guides, receiving their guidance with ease and grace."

Feel the presence of your Higher Self and guides, trusting their support throughout the session.

IDENTIFICATION OF LOST ENERGY

- "I command to identify any lost, scattered, or drained energy, whether from this life, past lives, or other dimensions."

- "I command to bring forth the memories, emotions, and circumstances surrounding the loss or scattering of this energy."

- "I command to reveal any unresolved situations, relationships, or events that may have caused this energy to be lost."

- "I command to understand the connections between this lost energy and my current life challenges, fatigue, or energy blockages."

Allow any images, feelings, or thoughts to surface. These insights may come through intuition, visions, or emotions.

RETRIEVAL AND RECONNECTION

- "I command to retrieve all lost, scattered, or drained energy, bringing it back to its rightful place within my being."

- "I command to dissolve any barriers, blocks, or resistance preventing the reintegration of this energy."

- "I command to heal and restore the connection between this retrieved energy and the core essence of my being."

- "I command to release any negative energies, attachments, or entities that may be associated with this lost energy."

- "I command to transmute all energies surrounding this retrieved energy into pure love and light, ensuring their safe and harmonious return."

Visualize the lost or scattered energy returning to you, merging back into your energy field, and bringing with it a renewed sense of vitality and strength.

HEALING AND REINTEGRATION

- "I command to heal any wounds or traumas associated with the loss or scattering of my energy, restoring harmony and balance within my being."

- "I command to integrate this retrieved energy fully, ensuring that it is aligned with my present life's purpose."

- "I command to restore my energy's integrity, bringing all aspects of my being into perfect unity and coherence."

- "I command to activate the vitality, strength, and resilience that this retrieved energy carries, enhancing my overall well-being."

- "I command to harmonize my energy field, ensuring that all retrieved energy is fully integrated and functioning in alignment with my highest self."

Feel the healing energy flow through you, replenishing your vitality and restoring your energetic balance. Imagine yourself absorbing the strength and vibrancy gained from this retrieval.

BALANCING AND HARMONIZATION

- "I command to balance and harmonize all energies within my body, mind, and spirit, ensuring alignment with my highest self."

- "I command to restore the natural flow of energy within my chakras, clearing any blockages related to the loss or scattering of energy."

- "I command to harmonize my present life with the retrieved energy, ensuring a smooth and effortless integration."

- "I command to anchor this new state of vitality and harmony into my daily life, allowing it to manifest in all areas of my experience."

Visualize your energy centers glowing brightly and spinning freely, in perfect alignment with each other. Feel the sense of renewed energy and balance settle into your being.

GRATITUDE AND CLOSING

- "I express deep gratitude to my Higher Self, spiritual guides, and the divine for their support and guidance during this healing session."

- "I command to close this session, sealing the healing and integration process with love and light."

- "I command to lock in all the positive shifts and transformations that have occurred during this session, ensuring they are permanent and lasting."

- "I command to gently disconnect from any energies or entities that are no longer needed, with gratitude and respect."

Take a moment to feel the completion of the session. Express your thanks and gently bring your awareness back to the present moment.

9.

SPIRITUAL CLEANSING WORKSHEETS

Spiritual cleansing is the process of purifying your energy and environment to release negativity and invite in positive, healing vibrations. This practice helps to clear away emotional clutter, energetic blockages, and any residual influences that may be weighing you down. Engaging in spiritual cleansing regularly helps maintain a sense of inner peace, clarity, and alignment, allowing you to feel more connected to your higher self and the positive energies around you.

HEALING SESSION NO: 36
ENTITY REMOVAL

SET THE INTENTION:

- "I set the intention to remove any and all entities, attachments, and negative energies from my being, energy field, aura, and space. I call upon my higher self, divine beings, and all protective forces to assist in this process with the highest good in mind."

GROUNDING:

- "I ground myself fully into the Earth, feeling stable, secure, and connected to the nurturing energy of Gaia."

PROTECTION:

- "I now call upon a protective bubble of white light to surround me, allowing only positive, divine energy to enter and remain."

IDENTIFYING PRESENCE:

- "I request the identification of any entities, attachments, or negative energies currently present in my energy field, aura, or physical space."

- "I ask for the identification of the source, nature, and any agreements or contracts related to these entities."

- "I command the identification of any hidden, cloaked, or suppressed entities or energies that may not be immediately apparent."

CLEARING THE ENTITIES:

- "I command that all identified entities, attachments, or negative energies be immediately cleared, dissolved, and removed from my energy field, aura, and physical space, without exception."

- "I command the nullification and cancellation of any agreements, contracts, or permissions that allowed these entities to attach to me, rendering them void and ineffective."

- "I command that all entities be escorted by divine beings to their appropriate place, whether it be the light or a suitable destination, ensuring they do not return."

- "I transmute all residual energy, fear, trauma, and negativity associated with these entities into pure love, light, and peace."

- "I command the purification of all energy centers, chakras, meridians, and any other parts of my being affected by these entities, restoring them to their perfect divine state."

SEALING AND PROTECTION:

- "I command the permanent sealing of all portals, gateways, or access points that these entities used to attach to me, with divine love and light."

- "I strengthen my protective shield, reinforcing it with divine light and a reflective surface that repels any future attempts of entity attachment."

- "I install a grid of protective light around my entire being, space, and any places I visit, ensuring continuous protection."

- "I command the restoration of my sovereignty and the reclamation of all my energy and power that may have been taken or lost to these entities."

- "I command the infusion of divine codes and frequencies into my energy field, ensuring alignment with the highest vibrational energy and protection."

RESTORING BALANCE AND HARMONY:

- "I command the recalibration of all my energy centers, aligning them with divine truth, love, and harmony."

- "I harmonize all aspects of my being, ensuring that every cell, every layer of my aura, and every part of my space vibrates with pure love and light."

- "I invoke divine healing, restoring any damage or imbalance caused by these entities, bringing my physical, emotional, mental, and spiritual bodies into perfect alignment."

- "I command the integration of divine light codes into my DNA, raising my vibration and ensuring continuous protection and alignment with my highest purpose."

FINAL CLEANSING AND REINFORCEMENT:

- "I command the cleansing and purification of all spaces, objects, and environments connected to me, removing any lingering or hidden negative energies or entities."

- "I reinforce all protections and ensure that all layers of my energy field are in perfect alignment and integrity."

- "I command a final sweep of my entire being, space, and environment to ensure that nothing unwanted remains."

CLOSING THE SESSION:

- "I affirm that this session is complete and that all entities, attachments, and negative energies have been fully removed, transmuted, and cleared."

- "I now close this session with deep gratitude, knowing that I am fully protected, aligned, and in harmony with my highest good."

HEALING SESSION NO: 37
CORD CUTTING

SET THE INTENTION:

- "I set the intention to sever all unhealthy, unwanted, or outdated energetic cords and connections that no longer serve my highest good. I call upon my higher self, divine beings, and all protective forces to assist in this process."

GROUNDING:

- "I ground myself fully into the Earth, feeling stable, secure, and connected to the nurturing energy of Gaia."

PROTECTION:

- "I surround myself with a protective bubble of white light, ensuring that only positive, divine energy can enter my space and being."

IDENTIFYING CORDS:

- "I command the identification of all unhealthy, unwanted, or outdated energetic cords connected to me, whether they are from past relationships, situations, or attachments."

- "I ask for the identification of the origins, nature, and impact of these cords on my physical, emotional, mental, and spiritual well-being."

- "I request the identification of any hidden, subconscious, or ancestral cords that may be affecting me."

CUTTING THE CORDS:

- "I command the immediate severance of all identified cords, completely and permanently cutting them from my energy field, aura, and physical body."

- "I revoke any agreements, contracts, or permissions that allowed these cords to form, rendering them null and void across all time, space, dimensions, and realities."

- "I command that any energy or power that has been drained or lost through these cords be returned to me now, fully cleansed and purified."

- "I ask for divine assistance in safely and effectively removing these cords, ensuring that no remnants remain and that the process is gentle and loving."

- "I command the transmutation of all energies associated with these cords into pure love and light, freeing me from any negative influence or attachment."

SEALING THE CORD SITES:

- "I command the healing and sealing of all sites where cords were attached, filling these spaces with divine light, love, and peace."

- "I reinforce these sites with protective energy, ensuring that no new cords can form in these areas."

- "I command the integration of divine codes of self-love, sovereignty, and empowerment into these spaces, strengthening my energy field and aura."

RESTORING BALANCE AND HARMONY:

- "I command the restoration of perfect balance, harmony, and alignment in my energy field and aura, following the removal of these cords."

- "I harmonize all aspects of my being, ensuring that every part of me vibrates with pure love, light, and divine truth."

- "I invoke divine healing to restore any imbalance caused by these cords, bringing my physical, emotional, mental, and spiritual bodies into perfect alignment."

STRENGTHENING BOUNDARIES:

- "I command the strengthening of my energetic boundaries, ensuring that only positive, loving connections take place as I move forward."

- "I reinforce my aura with a shield of divine light that repels any attempts to form unhealthy or unwanted cords in the future."

- "I command the installation of a divine filter in my energy field that allows only mutually beneficial and loving connections."

FINAL CLEANSING AND REINFORCEMENT:

- "I command a final sweep of my entire being, space, and environment to ensure that no unwanted cords, attachments, or energies remain."

- "I cleanse and purify all spaces, objects, and environments connected to me, removing any residual energies associated with these cords."

- "I reinforce all protections and ensure that all layers of my energy field are in perfect alignment and integrity."

CLOSING THE SESSION:

- "I thank my higher self, divine beings, and all protective forces for their assistance in this session."

- "I affirm that this session is complete and that all cords have been fully severed, transmuted, and cleared."

- "I close this session with deep gratitude, knowing that I am now free, empowered, and aligned with my highest good."

HEALING SESSION NO: 38
ENERGY DETOX

SET THE INTENTION:

- "I set the intention to detoxify my entire energy field, aura, and physical body, releasing and transmuting all negative, stagnant, or toxic energies into pure love and light. I call upon my higher self, divine beings, and all protective forces to assist in this process."

GROUNDING:

- "I ground myself fully into the Earth, drawing up its nurturing and purifying energy to stabilize and support me during this detoxification process."

PROTECTION:

- "I surround myself with a protective bubble of white light, ensuring that only positive, divine energy can enter my space and being."

IDENTIFYING TOXINS AND NEGATIVE ENERGIES:

- "I command the identification of all toxic, negative, or stagnant energies currently present in my physical, emotional, mental, and spiritual bodies."

- "I ask for the identification of the sources, origins, and nature of these energies, whether they stem from internal imbalances, external influences, or environmental factors."

- "I request the identification of any hidden, suppressed, or deeply embedded energies that may not be immediately apparent."

CLEARING AND RELEASING TOXINS:

- "I command the immediate release and clearing of all identified toxic, negative, or stagnant energies from my energy field, aura, and physical body."

- "I release all emotional, mental, and spiritual toxins that have accumulated over time, transmuting them into pure love and light."

- "I command the detoxification of all my energy centers, chakras, meridians, and any other parts of my being affected by these toxins, restoring them to their perfect divine state."

- "I command the release of all attachments, thought forms, or energetic imprints that contribute to the accumulation of toxins in my energy field."

- "I ask for divine assistance in gently and effectively purging all toxins from my being, ensuring a complete and thorough detoxification process."

PURIFICATION AND CLEANSING:

- "I command the purification of my entire energy field, aura, and physical body, filling every cell and every space with divine white light."

- "I cleanse and purify all layers of my aura, removing any residues, impurities, or blockages that may hinder my energy flow."

- "I command the purification of my surroundings, including my home, work space, and any environments I am in, removing all toxic or negative energies."

- "I ask for divine light to wash over me, cleansing and renewing my energy field, leaving me refreshed, revitalized, and in alignment with my highest good."

RESTORING BALANCE AND VITALITY:

- "I command the restoration of perfect balance, harmony, and vitality in my energy field and physical body, following this detoxification process."

- "I harmonize all aspects of my being, ensuring that every part of me vibrates with pure love, light, and divine truth."

- "I invoke divine healing to restore any imbalance or depletion caused by the accumulation of toxins, bringing my physical, emotional, mental, and spiritual bodies into perfect alignment."

- "I command the rejuvenation of my energy centers, infusing them with vitality, clarity, and divine life force."

STRENGTHENING IMMUNE AND ENERGY SYSTEMS:

- "I command the strengthening of my energetic and immune systems, ensuring they are resilient and capable of repelling any future toxins or negative energies."

- "I reinforce my aura with a shield of divine light, creating a protective barrier that filters and repels any harmful or toxic energies."

- "I ask for divine assistance in maintaining a high vibration and clear energy field, allowing only positive, nourishing energies to enter my space."

FINAL CLEANSING AND REINFORCEMENT:

- "I command a final sweep of my entire being, space, and environment to ensure that no residual toxins, negative energies, or impurities remain."

- "I cleanse and purify all spaces, objects, and environments connected to me, removing any lingering or hidden toxic energies."

- "I reinforce all protections and ensure that all layers of my energy field are in perfect alignment and integrity."

CLOSING THE SESSION:

- "I thank my higher self, divine beings, and all protective forces for their assistance in this energy detox session."

- "I affirm that this session is complete and that all toxins, negative energies, and impurities have been fully released, transmuted, and cleared."

- "I now close this session with deep gratitude, knowing that I am cleansed, purified, and aligned with my highest good."

HEALING SESSION NO: 39
AURA CLEANSING

SET THE INTENTION:

- "I set the intention to cleanse, purify, and strengthen my aura, removing all negative, stagnant, or unwanted energies. I call upon my higher self, divine beings, and all protective forces to assist in this process, ensuring it is conducted with the highest good in mind."

GROUNDING:

- "I ground myself fully into the Earth, feeling stable, secure, and supported by the nurturing energy of Gaia."

PROTECTION:

- "I surround myself with a protective bubble of white light, ensuring that only positive, divine energy can enter my space and being."

IDENTIFYING UNWANTED ENERGIES:

- "I command the identification of all negative, stagnant, or unwanted energies currently present in my aura, whether they stem from external influences, internal imbalances, or environmental factors."

- "I request the identification of any energies that do not belong to me or that are not aligned with my highest good, including attachments, thought forms, or imprints."

- "I ask for the identification of any hidden, suppressed, or deeply embedded energies that may be affecting the clarity and purity of my aura."

CLEARING AND RELEASING UNWANTED ENERGIES:

- "I command the immediate release and clearing of all identified negative, stagnant, or unwanted energies from my aura, completely and permanently removing them."

- "I release all energies that do not belong to me, sending them back to their source with love and light, ensuring they do not return."

- "I command the transmutation of all residual energies, emotions, or thought forms associated with these unwanted energies into pure love, light, and peace."

- "I ask for divine assistance in safely and effectively clearing my aura, ensuring that all layers are cleansed and purified."

PURIFICATION AND RENEWAL:

- "I command the purification of my entire aura, filling every layer with divine white light, cleansing and renewing it."

- "I cleanse and purify my aura from any blockages, impurities, or distortions that may hinder the flow of positive energy."

- "I command the renewal of my aura, restoring its natural vibrancy, clarity, and brilliance."

- I ask for divine light to infuse my aura, elevating its vibration and aligning it with my highest good."

HEALING AND RESTORING BALANCE:

- "I command the healing of any damage or imbalance in my aura, ensuring that all layers are restored to their perfect, divine state."

- "I harmonize all aspects of my aura, bringing every layer into alignment with divine love, light, and truth."

- "I invoke divine healing to restore the integrity, strength, and resilience of my aura, ensuring it fully supports and protects me."

STRENGTHENING AND PROTECTING THE AURA:

- "I command the strengthening of my aura, reinforcing it with a shield of divine light that repels any negative or unwanted energies."

- "I install a filter in my aura that allows only positive, nourishing energies to enter, while repelling any harmful or toxic influences."

- "I command the integration of divine codes and frequencies into my aura, ensuring it remains strong, vibrant, and aligned with my highest purpose."

FINAL CLEANSING AND REINFORCEMENT:

- "I command a final sweep of my entire aura, ensuring that no residual or unwanted energies remain."

- "I cleanse and purify all spaces, objects, and environments connected to me, removing any lingering energies that may affect my aura."

- "I reinforce all protections and ensure that all layers of my aura are in perfect alignment and integrity."

CLOSING THE SESSION:

- "I thank my higher self, divine beings, and all protective forces for their assistance in this aura cleansing session."

- "I affirm that this session is complete and that my aura is now fully cleansed, purified, and aligned with my highest good."

- "I close this session with deep gratitude, knowing that my aura is strong, vibrant, and in harmony with my true self."

10.

PAST LIFE GIFTS WORKSHEETS

Past life gifts are the abilities, insights, or talents that you bring with you from previous lifetimes into your current one. These gifts often manifest as natural skills, deep wisdom, or an intuitive understanding of certain subjects, even without prior learning or experience in this life. They can show up as strong affinities for specific cultures, professions, or practices, and often feel like second nature to you. Tapping into these past life gifts can enhance your personal growth and guide you on your spiritual path, offering valuable resources that help you navigate your current life with greater ease and purpose.

HEALING SESSION NO: 40
PAST LIFE TALENTS

INTENTION SETTING:

- "I intend to access and activate my past life talents that will serve my highest good in this lifetime."

CLEARING BLOCKAGES AND OBSTACLES:

- "I command to clear, release, and transmute all blockages, obstacles, fears, doubts, and limiting beliefs preventing me from accessing my past life talents into pure love and light. Remove any vows, contracts, or agreements that hinder my ability to connect with these talents, across all timelines, dimensions, and realities."

RELEASING KARMIC TIES:

- "I command to release and transmute any karmic ties, unresolved emotions, or negative energies associated with my past life talents that no longer serve my highest good. Allow only positive and supportive energies to remain, strengthening my connection to these talents."

OPENING THE CHANNEL:

- "I command to open the channel to my subconscious mind, higher self, and soul records, allowing me to access, retrieve, and integrate the skills, wisdom, and talents from my past lives that are most beneficial for me now. This connection is clear, strong, and aligned with my highest purpose."

ACTIVATING DORMANT TALENTS:

- "I command to activate all dormant talents, abilities, and gifts from my past lives that are aligned with my soul's purpose in this lifetime. These talents are now fully awakened, integrated, and expressed in ways that bring me joy, success, and fulfillment."

AMPLIFYING TALENTS AND ABILITIES:

- "I command to amplify and enhance the talents and abilities from my past lives, ensuring they are expressed at their highest potential. These amplified talents are now harmonized with my current life path and bring forth the highest outcomes in all areas of my life."

RECONNECTING WITH PAST LIFE KNOWLEDGE:

- "I command to reconnect with the knowledge, wisdom, and experiences of my past lives that can guide and support me in this lifetime. This reconnection is seamless and integrated into my conscious awareness, allowing me to utilize this wisdom effortlessly."

HARMONIZING ENERGIES AND TALENTS:

- "I command to harmonize the energies of my past life talents with my current life path, ensuring they are balanced, aligned, and supportive of my personal growth, success, and spiritual evolution."

MAXIMIZING OPPORTUNITIES AND SYNCHRONICITIES:

- "I command to maximize all opportunities and synchronicities where my past life talents can be expressed, utilized, and appreciated. These opportunities flow to me with ease and grace, bringing abundance, fulfillment, and joy."

STRENGTHENING CONFIDENCE AND TRUST:

- "I command to strengthen my confidence and trust in my past life talents. I trust in my abilities and know that they are valuable and needed in this lifetime. I confidently express these talents in ways that benefit myself and others."

HEALING AND RELEASING PAST LIFE TRAUMA:

- "I command to heal and release any trauma, fear, or pain associated with the use of my past life talents. I allow only the positive aspects of these talents to remain, fully integrated into my being and contributing to my well-being and success."

SEALING THE WORK AND SETTING FUTURE INTENTION:

- "I command that all the work done during this session is sealed in pure love and light, protected and aligned with my highest good. I set the intention for this work to continue evolving, ensuring that my past life talents grow and flourish as I do."

ANCHORING TALENTS INTO PRESENT REALITY:

- "I command to anchor my past life talents into my present reality, making them easily accessible and usable in my daily life. These talents are now fully integrated, supporting my highest good and contributing to my success, joy, and fulfillment."

CLOSING THE SESSION:

- "This session is now complete. I am grateful for the access to my past life talents, and I welcome their positive influence in my life. I trust in the process and know that these talents will unfold in perfect timing. So be it, and so it is."

HEALING SESSION NO 41

TRUE MISSION AND SOUL PURPOSE

INTENTION SETTING:

- "I intend to access and align with my true mission and purpose in this lifetime, in alignment with my highest good."

CLEARING CONFUSION AND BLOCKAGES:

- "I command to clear, release, and transmute all confusion, doubt, fear, and blockages that prevent me from accessing and understanding my true mission and purpose. This clearing occurs across all timelines, dimensions, and realities, and is transmuted into pure love and light."

RELEASING LIMITING BELIEFS:

- "I command to release and transmute any limiting beliefs, old programming, or past conditioning that obscures my awareness of my true mission and purpose. These beliefs are now dissolved and replaced with clarity, confidence, and alignment with my soul's path."

CONNECTING WITH HIGHER GUIDANCE:

- "I command to open and strengthen my connection with my higher self, guides, and the divine, allowing clear and direct communication regarding my true mission and purpose. This connection is now fully open, aligned, and protected."

ACTIVATING SOUL MEMORY:

- "I command to activate the memory of my soul's true mission and purpose in this lifetime. This memory is now fully awakened and integrated into my conscious awareness, guiding me with clarity and certainty."

ALIGNING WITH DIVINE TIMING:

- "I command to align with divine timing and flow, ensuring that I am always in the right place at the right time to fulfill my true mission and purpose. This alignment brings synchronicity, ease, and grace into every aspect of my life."

HARMONIZING LIFE PATH WITH MISSION:

- "I command to harmonize my life path with my true mission and purpose, ensuring that all aspects of my life are in alignment and support the fulfillment of my soul's purpose."

AMPLIFYING INTUITION AND INNER KNOWING:

- "I command to amplify my intuition, inner knowing, and divine guidance, making it easy for me to recognize and follow the path that aligns with my true mission and purpose. My intuition is now clear, strong, and trustworthy."

MAXIMIZING OPPORTUNITIES:

- "I command to maximize all opportunities and circumstances that allow me to express and fulfill my true mission and purpose. These opportunities flow to me effortlessly and support my growth, joy, and fulfillment."

CLEARING RESISTANCE AND FEARS:

- "I command to clear, release, and transmute any resistance, fears, or doubts about stepping into my true mission and purpose. These energies are now dissolved and replaced with courage, confidence, and trust in my divine path."

ANCHORING MISSION AND PURPOSE INTO REALITY:

- "I command to anchor my true mission and purpose into my present reality, making it tangible, actionable, and fully aligned with my daily life. This mission is now fully integrated and expressed in all areas of my life."

ENSURING CONTINUOUS ALIGNMENT:

- "I command to ensure that I remain continuously aligned with my true mission and purpose, no matter the changes or challenges I encounter. This alignment is strong, stable, and ever-present."

SEALING THE WORK

- "I command that all the work done during this session is sealed in pure love and light, protected and aligned with my highest good. I set the intention for this work to continue evolving, ensuring that I remain fully aligned with my true mission and purpose as I move forward."

CLOSING THE SESSION:

- "This session is now complete. I am grateful for the clarity, alignment, and connection to my true mission and purpose. I trust in the process and know that my path will continue to unfold in perfect timing. So be it, and so it is."

Past Life Dowsing

279

HEALING SESSION:

EFFECTS AND OUTCOMES

During healing and clearing sessions, the body and mind undergo a process of releasing stored energy and tension, often resulting in various physical and emotional manifestations.

- Yawning frequently during or after a session is a common response, indicating the release of stagnant energy and the body's natural attempt to rebalance itself.

- Some individuals may experience episodes of deep sleep or feel unusually fatigued, which can be interpreted as the body's need to integrate the healing energies and promote deep relaxation for optimal healing.

- Digestive changes like burping or mild diarrhea may also occur as the body detoxifies and eliminates toxins and emotional residues.

These symptoms are considered natural responses to the energetic shifts facilitated during healing sessions, reflecting the intricate connection between physical, emotional, and energetic well-being. It's important to honor these experiences as part of the healing journey and to allow the body to process and integrate the changes at its own pace.

Energy work involves the process of clearing away old, stagnant energies that have accumulated within the body and mind, while simultaneously integrating new, vital energies that promote healing and renewal.

- This transformative process unfolds gradually over time, typically resulting in noticeable changes within few seconds to few days to several weeks after a session.

- Initially, the release of stagnant energies may bring about temporary intensifications of negative states or symptoms as they are purged from the system.

- However, as the body adjusts and integrates the fresh influx of revitalizing energies, individuals often experience a gradual shift towards greater physical, emotional, and spiritual balance.

- This holistic approach recognizes that healing is a journey that varies for each person, influenced by factors such as their current state of health, resilience, and receptivity to change.

Through ongoing energy work, individuals can foster profound shifts in their well-being, ultimately enhancing their overall quality of life and inner harmony.

During energy work, if you encounter challenges in accessing healing energies, seeking assistance from guardian angels and your higher self can profoundly enhance your ability to facilitate healing.

- By inviting their guidance and support, you align yourself as a conduit and channel for universal healing energy to flow through you and into the client or patient.

- This practice acknowledges the spiritual dimensions of healing, allowing you to tap into higher realms of wisdom and divine energy sources.

- Engaging with guardian angels and your higher self not only amplifies your healing capabilities but also deepens your connection to the spiritual essence of the healing process.

- It transforms the session into a co-creative endeavor where you work in harmony with divine forces to bring about profound healing and transformation for the highest good of all involved.

This approach highlights the importance of spiritual alignment and intentionality in energy work, ensuring that healing energies are channeled with clarity, compassion, and effectiveness.

ABOUT THE AUTHOR

Minkal Vaishnav is a seasoned dowsing practitioner and author known for her insightful approach to spiritual healing and personal empowerment. With over a decade of experience in the field of dowsing, she started to develop her own unique strategies that combine intuition with deep energy work.

Her mission is to empower readers with the tools and knowledge needed to navigate life's challenges and complexities with ease and developing spiritual power within. She brings a unique blend of energy work and spiritual exploration to the field of dowsing.

Her books are alchemical workshops where subconscious wounds, past life trauma, energy blocks and harmful negative patterns are transmuted into healed, highest best version of self.

Her specialty is the use of pendulums, crystals and energy healing to assist those on their journey of awakening. Her primary focus is on teaching, practicing and sharing the ancient art of dowsing through her books and blogs. Her authentic, soul centered coaching style gently guides people to uncover their own wisdom and inner strength.

AUTHORS' NOTE:

DOWSING IS A CHOICE

Dowsing is a psychic gift, empowering one to engage with subtle energies and unveil hidden dimensions of their existence. By embracing the unseen reality of manifestation, dowsers embark on a personal odyssey of self-discovery and empowerment.

This journey unlocks their innate connection to the universe, enabling them to harness energies and uncover hidden truths about themselves and the world around them. This awakening creates a deeper understanding of existence and empowers them to alchemize their lives into purposeful and transformative expressions of their true potential.

Dowsing serves as a pathway to enhance one's psychic vision and senses, nurturing a deeper relationship with intuitive abilities. Simultaneously, it acts as a potent instrument for discernment, enabling individuals to identify and release energies, beliefs, or influences that do not align with their highest good.

Through dowsing, practitioners can selectively invite and cultivate energies and intentions that promote personal growth, well-being, and alignment with their truest potential.

My aim is for readers to develop a profound confidence in their dowsing abilities, grasp the underlying principles, and seamlessly incorporate this potent tool into their daily lives for invaluable guidance and insight. I envision a future where pendulum dowsing becomes a widespread practice, empowering individuals to effortlessly tap into their intuition and navigate life's problems with confidence and clarity.

As you close the final page, I invite you to persist in your exploration, practice diligently, and cultivate trust in your innate intuitive abilities. Pendulum dowsing is more than just a tool; it serves as a gateway to uncovering deeper layers of self-awareness and forging connections with the subtle energies that permeate our existence. Embrace this transformative journey with openness and curiosity, knowing that it has the power to enrich your life and expand your perception of reality.

Thank you for joining me on this journey and for your support and interest in my work. If you have any questions, stories to share, or just want to connect, please visit my website selfhelpdowsing.com and join my facebook page dowsing yoga. Thank you for taking the time to read this book and for your interest in pendulum dowsing. Your support means the world to me.

With gratitude,

Minkal Vaishnav

selfhelpdowsing.com

Printed in Great Britain
by Amazon